EXECUTIVE
IMAGE
POWER

Top Image Experts Share
What to Know
To Advance Your Career

D1125128

POWER**D**YNAMICS PUBLISHING

PowerDynamics Publishing
San Francisco, California
www.powerdynamicspub.com

ISBN: 978-0-578-01496-8

Library of Congress Control Number: 2009904688

Printed in the United States of America
on acid-free paper.

We dedicate this book to you, the CEO, salesperson or young professional just getting started, who knows the power of presenting your best possible image to advance your career. We know that you want to enhance your image and that you are ready to take positive steps to accelerate your career—and we celebrate you!

The Co-authors of Executive Image Power

Table of Contents

Acknowlegements

Gratitude looks good on everyone. Before we share our wisdom and experience with you, we have a few people to thank for turning our vision for this book into a reality.

This book was the brilliant concept of Caterina Rando, the founder of PowerDynamics Publishing and a respected image business strategist, with whom many of us have worked to grow our businesses. Working closely with so many image professionals, she realized how much she was learning about image and professional presence, and thought we should put our ideas into a book.

Without Caterina's "take action" spirit, her positive attitude and her commitment to excellence, you would not be reading this book, of which we are all so proud.

Additionally, all of our efforts were supported by a truly dedicated team who worked diligently to put together the best possible book. We are truly grateful for everyone's stellar contribution.

To Linda Jay Geldens, whose experience and expertise in copywriting, and in copyediting over 50 books proved very beneficial, and whose patience and flexibility was a true gift.

To LynAnn King, whose positive energy, big-thinking vision, public relations savvy and media expertise provided much-needed support, we are truly grateful.

To Ruth Schwartz, whose many years of experience and wisdom served as an ongoing guide throughout the project, your support is deeply appreciated.

To Barbara McDonald, who brought her creative talent to the cover design and book layout, thank you for your enthusiasm, problem solving and attention to detail throughout this project.

To Jeanette Vonier of Elegant Images, you truly are a master photographer. Thank you for working your magic quickly, allowing us to stay on deadline.

We also acknowledge each other for delivering outstanding information, guidance and advice. Through our work in this book and with our clients, we are truly committed to enhancing the image of professionals. We are truly grateful that we get to do work that we love and make a contribution to so many in the process. We do not take our good fortune lightly. We are clear on our mission—to make a genuine contribution to you, the reader. Thank you for granting us this extraordinary opportunity.

Introduction

Congratulations! You have opened an incredible resource, packed with great ideas that will enhance your career in ways you cannot yet imagine. You are about to discover the magic of *Executive Image Power.*

Your executive or professional image is so much more than getting a regular haircut, carrying a stylish briefcase and making sure your clothes are pressed. Your executive image is the message you send out to your clients, potential clients and colleagues every time you walk in a room, attend a meeting or talk on the phone. In fact, your executive image is the way you present yourself in all that you say and do! And of course, you want your executive image to be the absolute best it can be.

With this book, you can quickly rev up your executive image power, because as top experts in each of our respective specialties, we've joined together to give you the most powerful image strategies we know.

Each of us has seen how even small changes in your personal image can transform your self-confidence and uplift your career. A new custom-tailored suit boosts your self-assurance like nothing else.

Learning a few networking tips and knowing how to navigate a corporate cocktail party will ensure success the next time you attend a social business function.

Wearing colors that draw and hold the attention of others can help you make the right connections in your business or career.

Knowing how to use your silverware correctly, and mastering other dining etiquette details can lift you above your competition with poise and finesse.

All the image professionals you will meet in this book want you to present yourself in the best possible way. We have outlined for you our best tips, and the skills and strategies that can advance your career.

To get the most out of this book, we recommend that you read through it once, cover to cover. Then go back and follow the tips that apply to you, in the chapters most relevant to your current situation. Every executive image improvement you make will make a difference in how you feel and in how others respond to you in your daily professional life.

Know that just learning how to look your best will not transform your career. You must take action and apply the strategies, tips and tactics we share in these pages. Apply the many skills in this book and you will reap many rewards. With our knowledge and your action, we are confident that, like our thousands of satisfied clients, you too will master the magic of *Executive Image Power.*

To your success!

The Co-authors of Executive Image Power

Understanding Image Is Essential to Success

by Ginny Baldridge, AICI FLC

The image we choose to project to the world reflects who we are in every aspect of our careers. Sharing your expertise and wisdom through your image sends an authentic reflection of yourself.

Many professions have uniforms or standards of dress that represent the choices a person has made in life and the qualifications they have in their occupation.

In court, an attorney wears a suit, a sign of professionalism. The attorney does this out of respect for the judge, the client he represents and the court. When he shows up in court on your behalf, you feel confident that his many years of schooling and background make him the most qualified to represent you.

Similarly, a surgeon puts on scrubs before surgery. If the surgeon appeared just before a medical procedure wearing golf attire, you would have reason to be seriously concerned. The outward appearance of a professional should lead others to respond with confidence.

Surely clothing does not determine character, but it certainly affects what others think of us and how they respond to us. Think, for example, of a woman who is interviewing for a position as a bank loan officer. If she appears in a mini skirt, a low-cut blouse and dramatic makeup, her interviewer wonders if she is serious about the requirements of the position. Her dress and demeanor first affect the immediate senses and do not communicate the dynamic reality of her as a competent and loyal employee. On the other hand, picture a beautiful bride. Her dress and appearance communicate that she is a special person who loves and is loved. Her image engages both the mind and the heart.

The most distinguished and refined person in my experience was a frail little old woman, no more than four and one half feet tall. She was not beautiful by accepted standards—she did not dress lavishly. Rather, she dressed in the traditional simple attire of her profession. Her inner beauty was so magnificent that people passing by were drawn to embrace her. Her name was Mother Teresa. The way she lived her life made her a beautiful woman. A woman's femininity, her most attractive and fundamental quality, is enhanced if she is aware of her contribution to those around her.

In the United States, although 70 percent of women say that beauty is too narrowly defined by appearance, 90 percent of American women say if they had the funds, they would like to change something about their body through surgical measures. According to the International Society of Aesthetic Plastic Surgery, the United States is currently ranked number one in most plastic surgeries performed. Why the increased demand? For years, media outlets and women's magazines have defined outward appearance as the beauty of a woman. Reality TV has bombarded us with shows that demand that an average person be turned into a beauty queen. Lastly, advertisements on television, radio, billboards, magazines and the Internet attempt to persuade us that surgical "procedures" are the norm.

Attitudes about beauty and appearance vary, but the reality of image remains: at any given time, a dominant mode of dress reflects ideas about what it means to be a woman or a man in a particular culture. Historically, men were responsible for providing income, safety and direction for the family; the male professional image has changed very little over the years. But as women's roles have changed, so has their image, even though their inner qualities remain the same. Women are still the primary caregivers, intuitive to the needs of others, generous and self-sacrificing. A woman's image resonates so deeply within the human heart, it has the power to transform the tone of any situation.

Working with Professional Dignity

Here, then, is the challenge in cultivating one's career image: to rediscover image as an art that expresses true dignity and attractiveness, and to rediscover refined taste, which enables one to choose the specific style of dress that expresses one's individual personal and moral values.

Oscar de la Renta, famous apparel and fragrance designer, is a man who understands this very well. He said,

> *"Never before has woman had control of her destiny with the choices she makes and we should dress her with an elegant and feminine style."*

Unfortunately, as media saturates the world, we see too many unrealistic ideals. We are constantly inundated through television, movies and print media with images of celebrities. Many of us want to emulate these gorgeous people, but our own self-image may seem quite low by comparison, and we may have an impossible time measuring up to them.

In a recent interview in *GQ* magazine, Miuccia Prada, described as "the most powerful woman in fashion," had this to say about image:

"With women, the more unhappy, the more undressed they are....You have to have dignity for your body— this is with men and women. You need to have dignity towards how you are, how you dress, how you behave. Very important. Men are always much more dignified than most women."

Of course you always want to look your best. However, your best image includes practicing principles of integrity, charity, patience, humility, cheerfulness and other human virtues. If you were in a firm where these principles are practiced, you would sense this immediately. Consider walking into Tiffany & Co. You are greeted with a smile when you enter. Each employee is dressed in a professional suit and groomed to perfection. Each customer is waited on with patience and friendliness. The employee does not display a "superior attitude" but attends to you with genuine interest, whether you decide to purchase anything or not. The little blue box wrapped in a white ribbon is the company's unique image, true to Tiffany's commitment to the highest quality, style and customer service.

The notion of elegance remains central to the professional world today. The individual who lives with refinement and dignity as well as remaining approachable, reflects respect for himself or herself and others through attention to the little details of self-care. As you grow personally and professionally, it follows that your style of dress will change to mirror your character enrichment. Before we explore how to cultivate your best image on the outside, let's explore what you can do to enhance your inside, where your image begins.

Feeling Good Is Looking Good

In order to project an image consistent with our mission and goals in life, rejuvenation is needed. It is vital that we take good care of ourselves. Rejuvenation is described as: retreat, relaxation, renewal, make youthful, vigor, peace, health, longevity, to restore or make fresh again. Are you working so hard that there is never time to enjoy yourself or your family? Is the day filled with so much activity and stress that there is no time to rest or relax?

If we are able to focus on the body's true purpose, we will gravitate towards emphasizing health, fitness and enjoyment. Modern science continues to unlock secrets for living a longer and healthier life. Caring for our bodies with the benefits of exercise, hydration, healthy eating and a healthy lifestyle will help us feel energetic and rejuvenated.

Exercise Is Essential

Exercise is a key strategy in managing stress, staying rejuvenated and healthy. Exercise:

- Reduces the risk of all major diseases
- Increases mental vitality
- Maintains healthy heart and lungs
- Maintains healthy weight
- Increases bone density
- Increases energy
- Develops lean muscle mass
- Heightens self-esteem

One of the most important, and often overlooked, considerations in maintaining good health as one ages is exercising to build muscle. My best friend, who appears healthy, always joked that walking back and forth to the mailbox was her daily exercise. Of course that is not enough, because walking alone does not build muscle. Muscle is the powerhouse of the body where almost all energy is created by burning fat, carbohydrates and protein. Healthy, lean muscle mass is also vital to the immune system and reduces the risk of diabetes and osteoporosis. Fitness actually has nothing to do with torturing yourself on various exercise machines; instead, it is about helping your body to be the best it can be. Exercising your muscles with resistance training three to five days a week for 25-30 minutes will create energy and help you stay lean and strong for life.

Give Up the Soda

Seventy-five to eighty percent of Americans also suffer energy loss due to minor dehydration, which is a common cause of daytime fatigue. A dehydrated body is a stressed body. Drinking enough filtered water is essential, as every life-giving and healing process occurs inside your body. To neutralize the acidity of one glass of soda, it takes 32 glasses of water.

To determine how much water each day is right for you, take your body weight and divide it in half. That number is how many ounces of water you need to drink every day to stay hydrated and keep all the systems of your body working optimally. For example, if you weigh 150 pounds, you need to drink 75 ounces, or 9.3 eight-ounce glasses of water a day. You can drink a bit less if you eat a lot of water-dense foods like apples and oranges.

Nutrition That Counts

Generally speaking, most people are not getting enough whole-food, plant-based nutrition and are eating too much processed food. The science behind the health benefits of eating fruits and vegetables is exploding. There is no denying the research—fruits and vegetables prevent and even reverse disease. The skin reflects what you are or are not eating and reveals if waste products are retained in the body. Nutritional supplements cannot replace the hundreds of health-giving phytonutrients found in a single fruit or vegetable.

The Mayo Clinic Food Pyramid recommends seven servings of raw fruits and vegetables each day. So order a salad for lunch, take a banana in your briefcase for a snack; find new recipes that include raw fruits and vegetables, making sure you get your seven servings daily. As you heal your body and image, the effects will reverberate throughout your entire life.

Sleep Like a Baby

Sleep is absolutely essential for normal, healthy function. According to the National Institute of Neurological Disorders and Stroke, about 40 million people in the United States suffer from chronic long-term sleep disorders each year, and an additional 20 million people suffer occasional sleep problems. Sleep disorders include any combination of difficulty with falling asleep, staying asleep, intermittent wakefulness and early-morning awakening.

Studies show that sleep is essential for healthy cell growth, normal immune system function and maintaining the ability to fight disease. Sleep deprivation contributes to abnormal nervous system function, can cause daytime fatigue, depressed mood, anxiety, difficulty concentrating, apathy, irritability and complaints of decreased memory. Sleep is not a luxury, so if you do not wake up feeling rested, seek medical advice.

Most people need seven to nine hours of sleep to wake up feeling rested; you know how much sleep you need. One important way to combat sleep disorders is to go to sleep at the same time every night and awake at the same time every morning, creating a consistent sleep cycle for your body. Be sure you get enough rest and you will find you look better, feel better and are more productive every day.

Take Time for You

We can invite balance and harmony back into our mind and soul by taking better care of our inner selves. Many find waking fifteen to twenty minutes early in the morning and taking time for inspirations, prayer, meditation or journaling is a wonderful way to start the day. This time focused on self allows us to begin the day in a more serene and grounded way. Considerations for rejuvenation of the body include exfoliation, skin creams and lip gloss daily, along with spa or massage treatments as often as possible. It is never too late to slow down the process of aging and adopt an anti-aging lifestyle, which can keep your body looking younger for a longer time.

Take time every day to do those activities that you know support both your peace of mind and your body. Time you spend taking care of yourself is always time well spent, and your appearance will positively show that you are taking care of yourself.

Minimize Negative Influences

People and their negative energy and comments can certainly affect us. Evidence from *The Journal of Clinical Psychology* has proven that negative emotion is harmful to one's health, depleting both our physical vitality and our immune systems.

Emotional damage comes with many forms of negativity, such as news from the media, gossip at the office and constant complaining. Negativity depletes your energy levels, clouds your thinking and can put you in a bad mood. A co-worker may always see a glass as half-empty. Listening to her constantly complain about her responsibilities at work or her personal life can take a toll on you, the listener.

If a situation upsets or depresses you, try the method of *cancel, clear and delete.* This is a system of choosing to ignore a harmful situation, dismiss it from your mind and then forget it. In the case of the co-worker with the negative attitude, you would first stop the conversation with her and then begin a new task or converse with someone else on a happy topic, such as the score of a game that pleased you, or a great book you read or a movie you enjoyed. Then completely delete from your mind the conversation with the negative co-worker and move on with your day. Talk gently, think gently, and eat gently. Be gentle to yourself and others and watch how your stress dissolves.

Physical vitality can be improved with positive thoughts and activity. Our emotional well-being can easily be supported by a hug, which releases positive sensations into our body. Hugging or touching someone suffering with anxiety is supposed to generate hope, ease pain, convey care and give the receiver a feeling of being connected.

Humor also promotes health and wellness, as laughter is an excellent de-stressor and a therapeutic tool that can boost the nervous system. A smile looks good on everyone! When we learn to respect ourselves, take care of ourselves and pay attention to what we expose ourselves to, we can then begin to influence others positively. While you are making self-care an integral part of your life, constantly strive for balance in mind, body and soul.

The Impact of Attention To Your Image

Today, our leadership, expertise and authenticity are more important than ever to a successful professional image. Because we are living in uncertain times, influencing others to respond to us with confidence is crucial. Take the actions we have discussed to ensure you are communicating an image of someone who is healthy, takes care of themselves and is positive.

Focusing on your inner image will cultivate your best possible outer image. To the extent you invest in yourself, your health and well-being, you will see a valuable transformation occurring in both your personal life and in your career.

GINNY BALDRIDGE, AICI FLC
Your Style

*Helping people look and feel
great and achieve their personal
and professional goals*

(314) 952-8488
ginny@yourstyleginny.com
www.yourstyleginny.com

Ginny's valuable blend of personal experience and professional expertise has formed the foundation of her successful image business, Your Style. Her unique presentations focus on developing personal image consistent with strength of character, dignity and one's values. Your Style offers a diverse variety of programs ranging from quality corporate image training, business etiquette, entertaining and networking skills, to individual image coaching for success in your personal life.

Ginny holds a Masters of Education, is an Elegance In Style graduate, a member of National Speakers Association and is a certified member of the Association of Image Consultants International. Ginny regularly presents seminars to corporate clients, government employees, health care professionals, financial advisors, accountants, business and law associations.

As a mother of five and vibrant business owner, Ginny offers entertaining, energetic and inspiring guidance on any aspect of image.

Image Is Everywhere
The Power of Cultivating Your Own Personal Brand

by Lauren Solomon, MBA, AICI CIP

Image matters in business. Period. It communicates your success without saying a word.

Whether you are the new kid on the block, being groomed for your next big promotion, or president of your own firm for several years, your success depends on your being both the message and the messenger, inside the organization and out.

You are the Chief Executive Officer of your career. Whether you are at the head of the boardroom table or the go-to person who makes it all happen behind the scenes, get out in front of the team and lead with style.

In today's competitive marketplace, a brand image is not limited to commercial products sold to the consuming public via advertising and other marketing methods. You have a personal brand and your company or organization has a brand as well. Branding begins from the inside out, from the top down and from within the heart of the organization.

As a trusted image advisor, I have seen the significant difference enhancing your image makes personally on the inside with professionals as well as the huge impact it has outside within one's company and industry. Your personal image defines your professional image and your brand. Your image defines your world.

What does your image say about you and your company?

Are you aware of what you communicate before you ever reach out to kiss, bow or shake hands?

Could you unintentionally offend someone, damage a relationship, or, in the worst possible case, lose the promotion or the sale, due to image?

"You now have to decide what 'image' you want for your brand. Image means personality. Products, like people, have personalities, and they can make or break them in the market place."

—David Ogilvy, founder of Ogilvy & Mather and often referred to as "The Father of Advertising"

Establish your corporate leadership or career path with power and grace. A true leader delivers a message that will inspire, motivate and move to action. Prepare and present yourself with a magnetic style that connects from the heart. Position yourself, your team or your organization with respect and credibility in your industry and beyond.

Image Is For Everyone

Executives I have met over the years have told me that professional image consulting wasn't for them. It was for other people. It was for celebrities and politicians, people with smaller, taller or different bodies from theirs. They had a perception of image as glamour, sparkle and getting ready to walk the red carpet.

What they may not have realized is that they are on the red carpet every day in their business. Dressing for success isn't just for the Hollywood and television set. It creates the same impact, energy and attraction in your office or in the boardroom as it does at the Academy Awards.

Executives at all levels who embrace their image connect easily and effortlessly with the opportunities they seek, close deals more quickly and make a memorable impression on everyone they meet. Professionals tend to refer other professionals who make them feel good. People do business with people they like and trust. Collaboration comes from proven comfort, competence and clarity.

Cultivating your own personal brand is the result of your day-to-day decisions about what you think, how you feel, what you wear and the congruency of your overall presentation, not just what you say.

Develop your image from the inside out. Get clear about your corporate image and how you express this sincerely through your own authentic style and approach.

Be yourself, your best self. Explore what looks good on you and clean out what doesn't fit your personality, style and message.

Focus on raising the awareness of your corporate image by demonstrating its value to others, inside your organization and out in the marketplace.

Before Wardrobe and Beyond Beauty

You are the CEO of your life, whether you've just joined in, you are leading the team or it's your name on the door. This isn't a dress rehearsal. Every night is opening night. Image determines how you see yourself, and ultimately, how the world sees you and your company.

Image matters! Your image matters. It matters to everyone you meet, whether they tell you so or not.

Image is the gateway to your authenticity. Your unique way of being in the world emanates from how you speak, what you wear and how you feel, from the inside out.

When you cultivate your image strategically and deliberately, all doors will open before you.

Before you ever put on the clothes, there is a deep sense of who you are that sets you on your path to designing the right image for you.

"One of the greatest moments in anybody's developing experience is when he no longer tries to hide from himself but determines to get acquainted with himself as he really is."

—**Norman Vincent Peale, Author of** *The Power of Positive Thinking*

Overcome a lifetime of conditioning and become the most engaging person in every room. Deny your doubts and give change a chance.

No matter what size, shape, height or hair you have, your image is your highest and best investment in your career and yourself. Lose the wait and focus on winning from the inside out.

You need only look in the mirror to see that your outlook determines your outcome. By spending a bit of time with yourself to design and align your look with your intention, you'll quickly find that the real you will shine through in every situation with ease. You can start with these three easy steps:

1. Go to your closet. Select your "magic outfit"—the one you reach for when you have a really important meeting or have to dress-to-impress.

2. Identify the ingredients that make this your "magic" outfit. Is it the color? The perfect fit? The feel of the fabric? The confidence you feel wearing it? Or, is it the fact that you get positive feedback when you wear it?

3. Check yourself in a full-length mirror. Why isn't every outfit in your closet a "magic" outfit?

Take time for yourself to identify the look that introduces you without words. By looking good and feeling great every day, you give yourself a silent advantage over 95 percent of those you'll meet along your way.

Breaking The Sound Barrier

Stop, look and listen. Watch how others respond to you when you speak. Observe how your approach to a meeting and an important media interview are influenced by what you are not saying.

Your ability to show up, exude competence and inspire confidence communicates to all that you are fully prepared for every opportunity. Using your own words, innate charm and easy smile, distinguish yourself and your organization from the competition. On the big screen, small screen or face-to-face, drive your message, stay focused and have fun.

You may think that image is limited to your clothing, hair and makeup. Recognize that these are the translation, the external expression of the image and message that you project from within.

Congruency in what you say, wear and present to others instills trust, builds rapport and creates an understanding that is unspoken. Your message is the result of what you say and how you say it, successfully combined with what you don't say.

"I found that when you start thinking and saying what you really want, then your mind automatically shifts and pulls you in that direction. And sometimes it can be that simple, just a little twist in vocabulary that illustrates your attitude and philosophy."

—Jim Rohn, American entrepreneur, author and motivational speaker

Even in today's fiercely competitive business arena, connecting with others through clear, concise communication always wins. Whether you are talking with the media, presenting at a major industry conference, networking with other professionals, addressing your employee team, or meeting with a major client, by cultivating trust-based relationships, you stand up and stand out.

Mind Your Manners

"A man's manners are a mirror in which he shows his portrait."
**—Johann Wolfgang van Goethe, German playwright,
poet and novelist**

Etiquette is more complex in today's global economy and environment. Some circumstances are challenging, while others throw us so far off-balance that recovering seems impossible.

"Should I walk over and introduce myself?"

"Do I kiss, bow or shake hands?"

"Which bread plate is mine?"

"Should I send a thank-you note?"

"Which fork should I use?"

"Where do I leave my napkin if I get up to use the restroom?"

"Who should pay the check?"

See the chapters on *Networking Savvy from the Inside Out* by Brenda Moore-Frazier on page 137, and *Dining for Business Success* by Joanne Blake on page 149 to answer some of these questions.

Approach every situation with an aura of comfort, charisma and courtesy. Know what to do and understand the rules of engagement to leverage every interaction. Be of the world and make a lasting impression. Be an enjoyable host and a guest who always gets invited back.

*"Manners are a sensitive awareness of the feelings of others.
If you have that awareness, you have good manners, no matter
what fork you use."*
—Emily Post, etiquette icon

Know the rules, know when you can bend them and know when you can break them with confidence and style.

Overcoming Overwhelm

Capture the attention of an audience of one or one thousand. Master your authentic presentation style that people enjoy. Maximize each opportunity to share your meaningful message. Provide value and benefits to your audience every time. Present yourself clearly and sincerely, using a natural, genuine and accessible approach.

Transform frustrations into freedom of expression by simplifying your approach, organizing your image tools and techniques, and taking your personal and professional life to the next level.

Establish your presence and provide a deeper understanding through your expertise. Align your verbal and nonverbal expression and enhance your ability to engage your audience.

"It's not what you do once in a while, it's what you do day in and day out that makes the difference."

—Jenny Craig, founder, Jenny Craig Weight Loss Program

Take your internal, verbal message and translate it into a congruent, consistent, external, visual expression. From hair, eyewear and makeup to the stylish, coordinated outfits in your closet, save yourself time, energy and money, and simplify your life.

Corporate Advertising—Your Image At Work

Leverage every opportunity to communicate your corporate message clearly and succinctly. Introduce yourself with confidence and establish rapport quickly and easily.

Some executive clients have confided in me that they really weren't in a position to represent the corporate image because they weren't sure what it was themselves. How could they present something that was not perfectly clear to them? With whom could they discuss this dilemma and receive objective, non-judgmental insight to help them put their best foot forward and go beyond dress for success?

Defining a distinct, easy-to-understand message that reflects the essence of your business promise, vision and mission is the core of your corporate message. Make it concise and master your delivery of it.

Start by getting clear about your corporate message. What is it? Do you know for sure? Identify the following:

- The vision of the company
- Why the company exists
- The solutions the company provides
- The industry or people served by the company
- The expectations of your clients and industry

Invest the time to determine how to best align your own image with this important corporate communication tool. Turn your discerning eye toward your corporate team and discover whether you as a group represent the message your organization claims as its excellence in the marketplace. Now turn that discriminating eye on yourself.

Your image fills the gaps in your corporate message and eliminates the confusion in your overall presentation of yourself, your company and your global message.

The Top-Down Team Approach

Making the most of your own image is just the beginning. In business across America and on the world stage, you are not the sole representative of your organization.

"We changed our image. At least when we ran out on the field or broke the huddle, we would look like winners."

—Hayden Fry, National Collegiate Athletic Association college football coach and College Football Hall of Fame inductee

In any organization, employees are the most powerful brand ambassadors. Given the tools, skills and opportunity, you can represent your company and yourself with confidence and style.

Here are some simple things you can do to solidify your personal brand:

- Clarify one consistent message that applies to everyone
- Identify role models inside and outside your company who are winning in business and effectively representing themselves
- Align your look with theirs

Take a close look at your team and those around you. Evaluate how many of your colleagues may not be congruent with your company's message. Understand that, perhaps like you, they don't know where to begin or whom to ask for assistance. Some know and others may not realize they need help to look more consistent with the role they play in the organization.

Take an interest inside your company and focus on your team and colleagues. Develop their sense and sensibility to represent your organization with a unique style that complements your own.

Would a Change Do You Good?

After reading this book and focusing on your executive image, you may consider changing the image you have and crafting a new one.

If this is true for you, I recommend that you start from scratch. Assess who your company serves and how you play among the competition in the marketplace. Discover what truly sets your company apart from the rest of the players. Interview your clients and understand why what you bring to them is unique. Ask why they do business with you.

Evaluate the results of your inquiries and position your image on your company's strengths.

Align your inner message—what you stand for, the integrity of your products, service and staff, and how you serve your customers—with excellence and ease.

Build your world-class image on the core components of your message. Assemble your team and design your career path to support the implementation of your new winning approach. Express it in every possible way. Look the part. Communicate with confidence.

Refresh your message and master its delivery. From the top down and the inside out, your organization deserves another look at you and its corporate image.

Understand its impact and then coordinate yours.

Professionalism—The Ultimate Image

When colleagues say they enjoy doing business with you and your organization, you have converted your professionalism into profitability.

Not all executives know this secret ingredient to increase their success. Those who do, succeed in everything they do. Their image expresses their success, and it shows without ever saying a word.

*"Example is not the main thing in influencing others,
it is the only thing."*
**—Albert Schweitzer, Alsatian theologian, musician, philosopher
and physician**

Focus on strengthening all aspects of your career as leader, mentor and true chief executive of your life. Address all areas, including personal communication style, relationship building skills, occasion preparation, social savvy, team leadership and overall appearance.

Reap the rewards of your image investment. Radiate and celebrate your success.

LAUREN SOLOMON, MBA, AICI CIP
LS Image Associates

Your image matters—
it is your most powerful tool

(212) 873-1722
lauren@lsimage.com
www.lsimage.com

Lauren Solomon, MBA, AICI CIP, is the trusted image advisor to CEOs, millionaires and business start-ups alike. President of LS Image Associates in New York City and author of *Image Matters! First Steps on the Journey to Your Best Self,* she is the former Vice President of Professional Image Development at Chase Manhattan Bank; creator and lead instructor of the professional skills workshop, *The Brand Called Me*, at the New York University Stern School of Business; a faculty member of the Image Consulting Certification Program at the Fashion Institute of Technology; and President Emeritus of the Association of Image Consultants International.

Lauren is the Career TV image expert and an image industry spokesperson. She has been featured on Lifetime Television, MSNBC, CNN-fn, WOR and Voice America Women radio. She has also appeared in *The New York Times, New York* magazine, *Men's Health* magazine and other publications.

Solomon is the recipient of the AICI's 2005 IMMIE Award for Leadership and Professionalism (the highest professional honor) and the 1996 Award for Outstanding Achievement. She holds a Master of Business Administration from New York University and is certified in Image, Advanced Corporate Training, Interpersonal Communications, Business Etiquette, Color Analysis and International Protocol. Lauren is available for public and corporate speaking engagements and personal consultations.

The Power of Red, Yellow and Blue
Color's Importance for You

By Cynthia Bruno Wynkoop, Esq.

Color is *the* most significant aspect of visual professional image. Similar to the beautiful harmony of a well-played symphony, an individual in color harmony is a soothing and appealing sight and one to whom others are drawn. Conversely, just as one wrong note triggers a visceral negative reaction, an individual not in color harmony creates a visual distraction that affects their presence and their impact on others. This chapter discusses the fundamental principles of colors, their impact on the human body, and their use in the workplace.

As an image consultant, I am amazed by most people's lack of awareness regarding the impact of color on the human body. Even with an untrained eye, you can notice how fantastic a certain color can look on someone or how another color worn by the same person makes them look awful. By gaining an awareness of the power of color, you will enhance the way you look and the message you communicate to others.

Color Is Light: Light is Energy: Color is Energy

In the late seventeenth century, Sir Isaac Newton passed sunlight, or white light, through a prism, thereby discovering the visible spectrum. This array of six colors is composed of the three primary colors of red, blue, and yellow, and the secondary colors of orange, green, and purple. Sometimes purple is separated into indigo and violet, resulting in seven colors. Placed in order—red, orange, yellow, green, blue, and purple—each color travels to the human eye at different speeds and impacts the autonomic nervous system in vastly different ways. We not only see the color, but we also feel the energy associated with it. As an example, red, the fastest-moving color, is connected to primal aspects of our human existence—passion, sex, anger, power—that incite raw emotion. At the opposite end of the spectrum, purple, the slowest-moving color, not only soothes and relaxes, it also represents higher intellect and spirituality. Color is light, light is energy, thus color is energy, or the presence of life.

Did you know that a fascinating aspect of color is that it takes on the attributes of surrounding color in a process known as simultaneous contrast? The perfect illustration of this principle is the color periwinkle—a muted purplish-bluish color. Compared to a swatch of truer blue, periwinkle would become purple to the eye. Conversely, compared against purple, it would appear blue. Because the eye simultaneously contrasts Color A (in this example, periwinkle) against surrounding color, Color A actually changes its appearance to the eye, depending on the comparison being made. Through simultaneous contrast, colors both change their appearance and look better or worse. If two colors sit in harmony when simultaneously contrasted, each color looks truer and enhanced. If the two colors conflict, they battle each other. The result is that neither color looks its best; the dominant color becomes overpowering and the weaker is minimized. As discussed below, this principle has vast implications for color placed on the human body.

Although we classify the visible spectrum by six colors, we can combine these colors in an infinite number of ways, thereby creating new colors or hues. Each color can be darkened or lightened with whiteness or blackness, referred to as a color's value. Each color may also be softened or muted from its purest level of saturation, or intensity. Thus, we evaluate color based on **hue**—what we recognize commonly as the color's name—red, blue, green; its **value**—lightness or darkness; and its **chroma,** the degree of color intensity—or how much pure color exists. Through simultaneous contrast, colors that complement each other harmonize on all three levels, resulting in a picture of beauty for the human eye. Colors that do not harmonize detract from each other and create an unpleasant combination.

Nature continually harmonizes adjacent colors to produce remarkable, and often breathtaking, beauty. Envision pictures of the red, earthen muted tones of the Grand Canyon or the bright, vibrant colors of a tropical island to recognize that the earth's places we deem beautiful have colors that coordinate in appealing combinations. Regardless of nature's color scheme for that location, the colors of the earth, sky, water, and native plants and animals all harmonize to produce a unified whole. Although we appreciate this quality in nature, we frequently lose the ability to understand the impact of color on ourselves. Instead of maximizing our appearance with harmonious colors that complement our natural features, we detract from our appearance by wearing colors that create visual discord. While we do not have control over the genes that determine our color tone, we do have complete control over the colors we wear on our body to look our best.

Red, Yellow, and Blue—What Color Are You?

This chapter assumes that nature perfectly harmonized our natural coloring—hair, skin, and eyes. Skin is the largest organ of the human being. Impacting our skin tone either directly or through our bloodstream is a combination of three chemicals, melanin (blue), carotene (yellow), and hemoglobin (red). As a result, as with all things in nature, it is the combination of these primary colors of red, yellow and blue that dictates our skin tone. Consequently, it is this formula that we must understand and harmonize with in order to make the most of our physical appearance.

Think of a day when everyone commented about how great you looked, asking, "What did you do?" This can prove especially puzzling since that morning you did nothing different, and in fact, you may have done less than normal because you got a late start. The reason for your enhanced appearance is probably color harmony—the clothing you wore that day, particularly the color worn closest to your face, made you look your best.

More magical than any beauty treatment or cosmetic procedure, color harmony instantaneously achieves:

- Healthier looking skin
- Brighter eyes
- Reduced redness that is normally present in skin tone
- Reduced appearance of blemishes
- Reduced appearance of wrinkles and fine lines
- Appearance of weight loss

Conversely, unharmonious colors worn around the face create the appearance of:

- Older, less healthy-looking skin
- Deeper, more noticeable, fine lines and wrinkles
- Emphasized redness, blotchiness, and blemishes
- Hardness of features
- Appearance of weight gain

Through the principle of simultaneous contrast discussed above. the eye compares the color we wear near our face with our skin tone, resulting in either visual harmony or discord. When we are in harmony, the individual takes the leading role, with maximized appearance and with the support of color. If there is visual discord, "the color wears the individual" and either overwhelms them or underwhelms them. These principles even apply to hair color and makeup.

As children, we have an intuitive sense of which colors appeal to us. Left to their own devices, children will select the colors in which they look their best. Throughout our life, however, we are influenced by voices that skew our views on color altogether. The color noise most commonly begins with our mothers who, despite their best intentions, select colors based on their own misinformation and personal preferences. Closely followed by our friends, siblings, significant others, and the constantly changing colors promoted by the fashion industry and mass media, by the time we reach adulthood, we frequently have lost any intuitive knowledge of what colors are best for us.

To truly know what colors look best on you, have a personal color analysis done. All of the co-authors in this book either provide one-on-one color analysis or can refer you to a colleague who does. At our core, we have an innate desire to look our best—what we commonly define as having beauty. Though we most commonly associate this desire with attractiveness to a mate, beauty ties directly to our own self-confidence, empowerment, and success. Many studies describe a direct correlation between beauty and the ability to earn money. Beauty impacts directly the ability to obtain, retain, and advance in a job, as well as secure the salary and bonuses given by employers. That is not to suggest that skills, work ethic, and education are not significant; clearly, they play a fundamental role. All things being equal among similar candidates, those deemed more beautiful will achieve greater success in the workplace. Our natural desire is to interact with beauty, and those who are honest will admit that we possess biases for those we see as beautiful and against those we don't. Thus, it is in our best interest, for a multitude of reasons, to maximize our appearance. With color playing the most significant role in achieving this result, personal color analysis requires a nominal investment, but pays big dividends—quite literally!

In addition to the enhanced visual appearance of color harmony, our personality is closely associated with our coloring. This marriage of external and internal offers insight into personal traits and impacts how others interact with us. My favorite example of this is to compare Meg Ryan to Cher. Because most people personally do not know either woman, our impressions are based on their coloring and behavior. We find Meg Ryan inviting, with her All-American look characterized by hues of blue and yellow, lightness, and low–to-medium-intensity of color. She has a low-contrast look, consistent with her bubbly personality. People believe they could approach her easily at a cocktail party. Conversely, Cher, with her far more intense, dark coloring characterized by hues of red and purple, proves far more intimidating and not as approachable. Cher has a high-contrast look.

Someone with coloring similar to Meg Ryan may find that people naturally gravitate to them, but that they have to work harder to be taken seriously or to avoid serving as an emotional sounding board for others' problems. Someone with coloring more akin to Cher's may wonder why others label them as serious or intimidating, and why they have to work harder to seem inviting to others. In both instances, the answer lies in an understanding of personal coloring—both our visual image and the energy others attribute to it. Having this insight allows you the ability to maximize your interaction with others, both through the selection of complementary colors to wear and the comprehension of how your personal coloring affects others. What salesperson, litigator, or entrepreneur can afford to not understand how their coloring impacts the sale of their product, the effectiveness of their message, or the marketing of their company?

Like Meg and Cher, your coloring naturally contrasts somewhere along the spectrum from low-to-high. To maximize your appearance, recognize and embrace your innate level of contrast rather than attempting to alter it. That said, you can use colors within your color palette to create looks that contrast either more or less, depending on your primary objective for that day. On days when you need to exude power or authority, achieve a high-contrast look by wearing light colors from your palette in combination with dark colors. Although black and white offer the ultimate example of high contrast, should these not exist in your palette, you could try instead a more appropriate combination for you, such as navy and light blue, teal and ivory, or charcoal gray and pale pink. Conversely, for those days when you desire to become more inviting and approachable, select colors with more similar values to achieve a lower contrast look. Low-contrast examples include navy and burgundy, taupe and medium blue, or tan and cream.

Lastly, although readers should consult the *Closet R* chapter by Divya Vashi in this book on page 97 for specific information about closet organization, a color palette provides an essential platform for coordinating new clothing purchases with an existing wardrobe. The colors of the palette will harmonize with the individual, and also with each other. The result is a wardrobe with an infinite amount of mix-and-match options, all of which will maximize the individual's appearance.

Color in the Workplace

In your professional wardrobe, give careful thought to use of color. Your personal colors send messages and especially when you are in color harmony, the color of your clothing transmits messages. The use of color will make or break your appearance; an individual should use color in ways that are appropriate and consistent with their professional objectives.

In addition to maximizing appearance, an individual savvy in both personal color palette and color principles can use color as stagecraft. For example:

- A salesman can select a shirt color based on the pleasant impact on his face, but also the calmness it brings to disarm potential customers.
- A financial executive trying to close a high-stakes deal can select a suit color to communicate trust and reliability.

- A woman offering a lecture to an audience may select a harmonious shade of red lipstick to help listeners focus on her mouth, and the words she is speaking, to maximize the impact of the talk.

- A litigator may dress his client in color harmony to make a statement of wellness, or in color discord to offer a picture of his client's ill health, depending on the theory of his case.

In a perfect world, we could all dress for work in harmony with our individual coloring, but many work environments do not provide this flexibility. As one example, the traditional environments of the financial and legal professions limit the freedom of color expression. An individual working in this type of environment is ill-advised to show up for work in a lime-green garment, regardless of color harmony. In fact, lime-green should be limited to a cameo appearance in a tie, scarf, or other accessory (cufflinks, a pendant). A work environment requiring a uniform or prescribed dress focuses on sameness and building esprit de corps. As such, the individual in this work environment needs to accept these constraints during the workday and focus on color harmony and expression in other areas of their life.

Color offers an unequaled ability to instantly achieve an appearance of wellness and beauty that contributes directly to esteem and achievement. Understanding the colors that are in harmony with you, and how to use them to achieve professional success, is critical. Invest in a personal color analysis, begin the journey of understanding your personal coloring, and appreciate the ability to realize your most beautiful, your most accomplished, your most powerful you!

CYNTHIA BRUNO WYNKOOP, Esq.
Wynkoop Image

Image is more than beauty

(559) 593-1471
cynthia@wynkoopimage.com
www.wynkoopimage.com

After successful careers as a lawyer and a corporate executive, Cynthia followed her true passion of empowering people and assisting companies to achieve success through image. Drawing from her years of professional experience, Cynthia believes that image is less about beauty than about projecting success and desirability specific to the objectives and integrity of the individual or company—we first have to feel attractive and resonate attraction to attract our desires! She works with clients to understand their unique objectives and achieve an image consistent with these goals.

Cynthia has worked with corporate clients in the fields of law, healthcare, insurance, real estate, and media to build professionalism by creating dress standards and educating employees. Cynthia has served a cross-section of private clients from stay-at-home moms to CEOs, a political candidate and a newscaster. Cynthia works with litigation attorneys to develop appropriate visual images for the litigation team and client to maximize "likeability" and advance the theory of the case.

Cynthia possesses a specialization in the field of color and the human being. She maintains memberships in the Association of Image Consultants International, the Sci/Art Network of color analysts, and the California Bar Association.

Capsule Dressing for Men and Women
How to Have an Easy Wardrobe

By Karen Brunger, BHEc, AICI CIP

Capsule dressing can facilitate and enhance your professional success. It allows you the flexibility of an appropriate, coordinated look for any situation, whether it's a high-powered meeting, a day in the office, a lunch with friends or a cocktail party. It enables a higher-quality, more prestigious image; since fewer pieces are required, your wardrobe investment has more impact. Capsule dressing facilitates wardrobe organizing, planning and shopping, and lets you create a wardrobe that is effortless and timesaving.

Paul's Story

As the president and owner of a business specializing in information technology, Paul sells his products to CEOs of Fortune 500 companies. One CEO told Paul that he should see an image consultant, as he was sabotaging his business. Paul became my client. As a technology person, he had not factored his image into the equation of promoting his product. So, his image was uncoordinated, unprofessional and unflattering. His clothes were put together with no consideration for color, fabric or appropriateness.

We quickly discarded about 95 percent of his wardrobe, then developed some wardrobe capsules that would allow him to be comfortable, appropriate and credible, not only for his important meetings, but for all facets of his life. The colors, fabrics, and styles suited his body type, coloring and personality.

A month after we got him started on his first capsules, I received a telephone call from Paul. He was almost speechless, he was so overcome. He said, "I can't begin to tell you the difference that this has made in my life." He reported that his income had tripled, his staff was now treating him with more respect—and the biggest thrill? Women were approaching him!

The great news is that anyone can achieve this dynamic, cohesive and effortless image and wardrobe. Capsule dressing is an easy-to-use wardrobe system that can enable you to:

• Save time, money and space.

• Have something for every occasion.

• Create a "put together" look at all times.

• Eliminate frustrating wardrobe shopping and costly mistakes.

A capsule is a collection of clothing in which each item can be coordinated with the others, creating complete, pulled-together outfits.

Capsule dressing involves a total of eight steps spanning three areas of focus:

• Lifestyle analysis.

• Capsule planning.

• Capsule coordinating.

Lifestyle Analysis

Your wardrobe capsules should serve your current functions and help you achieve future goals. The chart on the following page lists different lifestyles and typical functions for each.

Step 1. Identify the lifestyle categories in which you plan to be involved within the next two years. List the categories in the chart on page 38.

Lifestyle	Typical Functions
Formal Business	High-level meeting; presentation.
Business	Day-to-day business; meeting; networking.
Business Casual	Desk work; teaching; networking.
Smart Casual	Creative work; sightseeing; traveling.
Casual	Shopping; school; visiting; spectator sport.
Active and Leisure	Exercising; lounging; housework.
Evening Informal	Clubbing; casual date.
Evening Semi-Formal	Cocktail party; wedding.
Evening Formal	Gala; ball; black-tie.

Step 2. List the approximate number of hours you would spend in each lifestyle in a typical week. It's easiest if you round the number up to the nearest 10. For each lifestyle that does not occur every week—for example, Evening Formal—assign 10 hours.

Now that you have established how your time is spent, you can calculate the capsules you require. The formula is:

10 hours = ½ capsule
20 hours = 1 capsule
30 hours = 1 ½ capsules
40 hours = 2 capsules and so on.

Step 3. List the number of capsules you require for each lifestyle.

Lifestyle/Function	Hours/week	Capsules

When you add together the total number of capsules that you require, it will probably be at least 5, but should not be more than 10. I have cleaned out some closets where there were enough clothes for 30 capsules!

Maria's Story

Closet chaos and clothing catastrophes described Maria's situation. A sales consultant, Maria was told by her supervisor to seek the services of an image consultant. Maria emphasized over and over, "I have no clothes, because I have no money. I can't afford to buy new clothing." After six hours of steady closet cleaning, we had barely made an impression in the cavern she called a closet. It was still filled to overflowing, even though our cast-offs could have filled a Mack truck.

Although Maria had "no money to buy clothes," every week she'd been buying a clothing item for $5 or $10. The result was a mountain of garbage-garments. If Maria had taken the same amount of money and used our capsule system, she could have been wearing high-end designer clothes.

Although this was an extreme situation, I've had a similar experience with many clients. They apologize for having no clothing, but they actually have enough items for numerous capsules. The problem is—very little, if any, can be coordinated together into outfits.

Capsule Planning

A sample capsule chart is below. Use this as a guideline for your capsules.

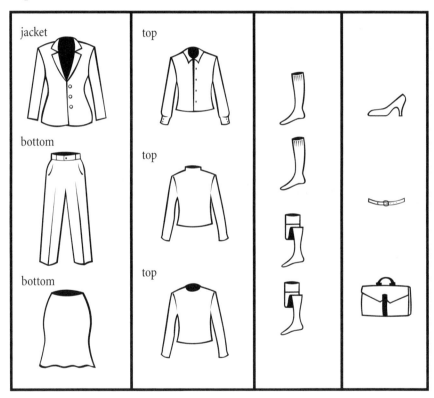

Step 4. Create your personalized capsule charts.
Set up blank charts, using the above formula, for your own capsules. Each capsule can have its own page. Label each capsule with the appropriate lifestyle. If you need clothing for both cold and warm weather, also label each category with the appropriate season.

Capsule Items

Step 5. Choose the items appropriate for each capsule.
Business requires suits, so an extra jacket is added. For women, skirts are dressier than trousers; use skirts in your business capsules. For men, in your business capsule incorporate five ties. For women, with each skirt or trouser, include at least two pairs of appropriate hosiery.

Capsule Colors

Step 6. Label each capsule with a projected color palette.
Each capsule should have one to three colors that coordinate. Use colors that harmonize with your own natural coloring. Neutral colors are long-term and are good for investment items. The higher the contrast between a suit and a shirt, the more professional. The darker, colder and more neutral the color, the more powerful and authoritative.

The chart below can help you choose the most appropriate colors.

Colors	Image
Neutral—dark and cold Black, gray, navy	Professional, authoritative, powerful, formal, sophisticated, conservative.
Neutral—light and warm Brown, taupe, tan, camel	Professional, elegant, practical, sincere, calm, inviting.
Light Ice white, soft white, ivory, eggshell	Light-hearted and open in a casual outfit. Professional and sharp in a business shirt. Elegant in an evening outfit.
Basic Green, blue, purple, burgundy	Creative, comfortable
Accent Red, orange, yellow, fuschia	Active, fun, noticeable, advancing, outgoing, warm, vibrant.

For more about selecting the best colors for your capsules, see Cynthia Bruno Wynkoop's chapter on *The Power of Red, Yellow and Blue: Color's Importance For You* on page 25.

Capsule Fabrics. Use appropriate fabrics for each lifestyle. The finer and silkier the fibers, the more elegant and dressy the fabric. Match the refinement of the fabric to the end use of the garment. Highly refined fabrics are used for business dress and elegant evening. Moderately refined fabrics are used for business casual and informal evening. Low refined or rustic fabrics are used for casual. The fabrics do not need to be listed on the capsule charts. However, they will need to be taken into account when coordinating your wardrobe.

Lifestyle Wardrobe Details. Here are some additional details that may help you develop capsules appropriate for lifestyles.

Formal Business	Color	Material
Suit	Dark, cold, neutral: navy, charcoal, black	Fine wool; solid or pin stripe
Shirt	White, cream	Highly refined cotton. Low-sheen silk acceptable for women
Tie	Burgundy, blue, grey, gold	Silk; solid, pin dot, rep, medallion
Pocket Square	White	Linen

Business	Color	Material
Suit	Neutral or dark	Fine wool; solid, pin stripe or subtle check
Shirt	Pastel or stripe	Highly refined cotton. Low-sheen silk acceptable for women
Tie	May match your personal coloring	Silk; may be stylized or abstract
Pocket Square	May pick up a color from the shirt or tie	

Follow the guidelines below when selecting your capsule items for each of the different lifestyle categories.

Business and Formal Business.

- **Suit.** Sharply tailored and classic. For women, skirt suits are more professional than trouser suits.

- **Shirt.** Classic with long sleeves and a collar.

- **Shoes.** Oxfords for men; classic pumps for women.

- **Hose.** Men: executive length matching trouser color. Women: sheer skin-tone hose.

- **Belt.** Classic leather, matching the shoes.

- **Jewelry.** Gold or platinum; classic, understated, and professional.

- **Pen.** Good quality and elegant.

- **Briefcase.** Good leather; the narrower, the better.

- **Eyewear.** Neutral; a classic style with non-reflective lenses.

Business Casual

- A jacket coordinated with trousers or skirt, or a suit in a non-business style.

- Texture and pattern can be stronger than at the business level.

- Colors can be lighter, softer, brighter and warmer than at the business level.

- Footwear may be less corporate, such as a loafer.

- Individuality can be slightly more expressed.

Smart Casual

- A sweater may replace the jacket.

- Textures, colors, and patterns can be more distinctive and relaxed than in Business Casual.

- Fabrics may be more medium-level refinement—tweed, corduroy, knits.

Casual

- Fabrics can be more rustic—suede, leather, denim, chunky knits.
- Styles are more relaxed—shorts, T-shirts, sandals.

Active and Leisure

- Clothing is appropriate for the beach, exercise or at-home.

Evening Informal

- Clothing is sensual, but casual.
- Fabrics may have some evening detail, such as sheen.

Evening Semi-Formal

- Men wear a dark suit with shirt and silk tie.
- Women may wear a cocktail-length dress; shoes and evening bag are shiny or match the outfit. Jewelry is glittery.

Evening Formal for Men

- Suit is a black evening or tuxedo suit; a cummerbund or waistcoat is optional. In hot weather, the dark suit may be replaced with a white dinner jacket.
- Shirt is white fine linen or cotton; it may have French cuffs for cufflinks, and use studs rather than buttons. The collar may be wing or standard.
- Tie is usually black—either a bow or regular.
- Shoes are black evening slip-ons or lace-ups, usually in patent leather.
- Socks are sheer black.

Evening Formal for Women

- Gown is full-length.
- Shoes and bag are evening.
- Jewelry is glittery.

Creating the Outfits

In coordinating your capsule combinations, the more related the design elements, the easier they are to combine. Here are some obvious matches:

Scale refers to size.
Small with small.   Large with large.

Dimension refers to thickness.
Fine with fine.   Chunky with chunky.

Line refers to lines within the design.
Straight with straight.   Curves with curves.

Shape refers to the outline of a design.
Angular shapes with angular.   Rounded shapes with rounded.

Texture refers to the look or feel of the fabric.
Sheen with sheen.   Matte with matte.
Smooth with smooth.   Rough with rough.
Soft with soft.   Hard with hard.

Pattern refers to a printed design, such as a check or a paisley. When a solid is combined with a print, the solid picks up a color from the print. For example, a navy-and-red patterned jacket would be worn with navy or red.

When two or more patterns are combined, the more they have in common, the easier they are to combine. The patterns can relate in scale, dimension, shape, texture, or color.

Colors

When combining solids, use no more than three colors. When two or three solids are combined, then the secondary and accent colors appear two or three times. The dominant color may appear more than three times.

Generally, darker colors are kept lower—such as shoes—and lighter colors are kept higher. Belts and bags tone with shoes, and may be lighter. The eye goes first to the lighter or brighter color.

George's Story

George is a psychiatrist. He loves the outdoors and engages in numerous outdoor sports and activities. His goal was to start a business in a new, somewhat glamorous industry.

George's wardrobe consisted entirely of well-worn and worn-out rugged outdoor active-wear. Although he had the face and body of a romantic hero, they were hidden under a scruffy exterior. He needed help!

As George had a good income and needed a more polished image, it was easy to find capsule coordinates that flattered his deep autumn coloring.

The difference was stunning. His charisma and dynamic personality were enhanced. He got a girlfriend. He achieved his goal of starting a new business. He bought his dream car. And, he said everything was a result of his new image!

Capsule Coordinating

Now that you have planned the details for each of your capsules, let's start putting them together.

Step 7. On your capsule charts, place a ✓ beside the items you already own.

Step 8. Decide which items or capsules need to be purchased at this time. In most cases, it is advisable to buy no more than one capsule per season. For example, you may purchase one-half of a professional capsule and one-half of a casual capsule.

Your Wardrobe Financial Investment

The wardrobe financial investment suggested here would be appropriate for an economy similar to the United States and Canada.

The suggested annual clothing investment for all clothing items—including underwear, outerwear, and accessories—is based on your gross annual income, or the gross annual income that you would like to achieve.

If Your Lifestyle is Predominantly...	Your Investment Would Be...
Casual	3-4%
Business Casual	5-6%
Business	7-8%

How much should you invest in each item? Let's use a business suit as the guide. The cost and quality of other items would then fall in line accordingly.

Joann is vice president of a bank and wears a suit every day. Her suit would be 1.2 percent—1.5 percent of her gross annual income. Leslie is a consultant and wears a suit once a month for meetings. Her suit is 0.8 percent—1.2 percent of her gross annual income. Gordon is a farmer and rarely wears a suit. His suit would be 0.5 percent—0.8 percent of his gross annual income.

The average duration of a well-made garment is five years. The higher the refinement and quality of the clothing, the longer it will last. Cold weather's heavier weight clothing may last longer than hot weather's lighter weight clothing.

Where to Shop

Select the appropriate stores based on price points. Look for the highest quality possible for the price range. Sales or discounts can offer good value, but not always the best choices.

If you have a challenge purchasing ready-made, you may choose custom or semi-custom. With custom—also called bespoke—the garment is fit to the body during a series of fittings. With semi-custom, the garment is cut from a standard pattern and altered to your measurements before it is assembled.

The advantage of custom or semi-custom is that you control the color, style, fabric, workmanship and fit. Especially for suits, if you are not easy to fit with ready-made, your best choice is custom or semi-custom.

Capsule Combinations

Working with capsules can allow you to build a large wardrobe to handle a variety of situations, based on a few pieces. Here are the number of outfits that can be created from capsules of five items—one jacket, two bottoms, three tops. The number of outfits depends on how the items can be combined.

If you like mathematical formulas, and you would like to calculate the number of outfits in your wardrobe, here is my formula:

$$(B \times C) + (B \times J \times T) - (B \times S)$$

B = bottoms

The other letters are tops, jackets and sweaters that can be worn:

C = alone

J = over something else

T = under something else

S = alone and under and over something else

Number of Capsules	Number of Outfits
1	6-18
2	12-120
3	18-378
4	24-859
5	30-1,650

Even if you have some items that are limited in their coordination potential, you can still achieve a wide range of looks.

Helen's Story

Helen is an investment banker with whom I worked on optimizing her image and wardrobe. Helen had a dilemma typical of most of my clients. She had "nothing to wear."

When I went through her closet, Helen actually had enough clothing for approximately 50 capsules. The problem? Nothing coordinated. She had also invested in low-quality clothing, which sabotaged her confidence, professionalism and credibility.

Within a year of working with me, Helen had a coordinated wardrobe that showcased her credentials and outgoing personality, enhanced her coloring and physical features, and allowed her to be pulled together and comfortable for any situation. She shared, "I spent exactly the same amount on my wardrobe this year as last year. The difference is, at the end of last year, I had nothing to wear. At the end of this year, I have clothing for any occasion that is inspiring and empowering."

Build your own wonder wardrobe. Coordinate through capsules, and make getting dressed easy, inspiring, and empowering. Capsule dressing will save you time and money and best of all, you will look great and feel confident in every situation.

KAREN BRUNGER, BHEc, AICI CIP
International Image Institute Inc.

Recognize potential,
embrace possibilities,
and intensify personal power

(905) 773-6599
karenbrunger@imageinstitute.com
www.imageinstitute.com

Karen Brunger is a recipient of the Award of Excellence, and the Who's Who Canadian Woman of the Year. International President of the Association of Image Consultants International for 2007-2009, Karen also served as international VP Education for four years. A pioneer in the industry, her in-depth knowledge and broad experience span twenty-five years.

As a holistic image consultant, Karen facilitates authentic transformation. She has optimized the personal and professional development of more than 2,000 individuals on appearance, behavior and communications to ensure they achieve more of what is possible. She draws on a variety of models, including neuro-linguistic programming and energetic repatterning. Her private clients have included executives, entertainers and politicians.

A dynamic, engaging and inspirational keynote speaker and trainer, Karen has conducted corporate seminars and workshops for many Fortune 500 companies.

As an international trainer, Karen has coached some of the top consultants in the industry. The producer of numerous workbooks and tools for image consultants, her systems and products are currently in sixty countries.

Media-trained, and a regular guest expert, Karen has appeared in hundreds of print and broadcast media within Canada and internationally. She is a regular contributor to *B Magazine.*

Executive Style
Unlock Your Power Image

By Beth Thorp, AICI CIP, CMB

To begin the journey on executive style, you must first ask yourself some personal questions. What business image do you project? How do others perceive you? How do you perceive yourself? What is the message you want to send? What would your clothes and grooming say to those in a position to give you a promotion or a contract? Take a moment and write down your answers. If you are unsure about these responses, ask a friend, trustworthy co-worker or long-term client for their thoughts on your professional business image, then compare "what is" to "what you would like it to be."

Careers are built upon daily tasks and lasting impressions. Imagine that every day is an interview for the next step in your professional life, and that your clothes, grooming and mannerisms have the potential to convey messages that promote rather than prevent future opportunities.

First Impressions Matter!
People pass judgment in seconds, categorizing "what they see" as either acceptable or unacceptable. Expectations are established, shaping character, self-confidence, enthusiasm, future paths and the compatibility of your personality conforming within an established work environment. Appear honest yet unique, flexible enough to complement others within a group. Be authentic in your approach,

try not to be someone or dress like someone you're not, which will inevitably send a negative impression. Dressing appropriately for the office is a sign of respect. It shows that you respect yourself, and others will as well.

Albert Mehrabian, the famous behavioral psychologist from UCLA, identified the importance of personal appearance through one of his studies, *Verbal, Vocal, Visual,* in 1971. He determined that first impressions are based 55 percent on how you look, 38 percent based on how you speak, and 7 percent on what you say. This proves the power of your executive presentation. With this in mind, dress always for the position you aspire to achieve.

In this chapter I define what Business Tailored, Business Smart, Business Casual and Weekend Attire should look like, and the messages they send. I will share with you tips on how to develop your own signature look suitable for your career, lifestyle, age and personality.

Applying these business styles to guide your selections empowers you to project an appropriate image and convey a positive message. It will add power and presence, and assure confidence for any business or social situation. Remember, image management is all about YOU taking control of the messages that you send out to the world.

Every industry has particular dress standards, whereas divisions within the same company may call for different attire. Inquiries regarding a company's dress culture should be directly addressed before a personal interview occurs. The dress code provides some insight, but important decisions regarding your clothing and grooming choices are still to be made. How do we make appropriate choices that convey a positive message to future employers? I include some basic guidelines that never go out of style.

1. **Appropriate.** An office is like a club. Look like you belong, not like you're an outsider. Dress age-appropriate as well.

2. **Professional.** Determine whether your industry is corporate or casual dress, and follow the executive style guide on the following page.

3. **Comfortable.** Decide how to properly dress your body type, your coloring and your personality. Remember, comfortable does not mean sloppy.

4. **Strategic.** Clothes attract attention. Ask yourself if you want your boss to notice you more. Observe how he or she dresses and follow their lead. However, if you don't like what you see, look around at your other coworkers to see what is acceptable. Avoid extreme looks, either formal or casual, if you want to be viewed as a team player. The goal is to stay within the parameters of your dress code within your work environment.

Coordinate your business wardrobe with your business calendar. Different work situations require different messages. Look at your business schedule the night before so you can properly plan your dress. For example: 10 a.m. staff meeting—I want to project approachable and strong; 1 p.m. Lunch with CEO—I want to project polished and management material; 5 p.m. networking event—I want to project approachable and relaxed.

Remember, constructing a polished business wardrobe is as important as crafting a business letter or proposal . . . they both require time and attention.

I recently attended an international conference where the dress code for each event was defined. This is a great help for those who are confused about what to pack or wear for business events. However, it may cause a problem for those who don't understand exactly what Business Tailored, Business Smart, Business Casual and Weekend Attire mean. Let us begin by following this chart as a resource to determine your own Executive Style Guide™.

Business Tailored: Most Formal

Key detail: Matching suit for men and matching suit with skirt or dress for women.

Occasions	Message Cues	Design Details	Examples
Company meetings, board meetings, major sales calls, presentations, overseas, conferences.	authoritative knowledgeable organized efficient trustworthy	Matched suit for men and women. A dress or skirt for women. Shirt and tie for men.	
Entertaining a client at a formal restaurant, either dinner or lunch.	formal manner precise persuasive credible	Straight angular lines and shape. Classic styles. Darker colors.	
Wear when you need a power look.	more formal stable official	Quality fabric, like super 100's or higher. Solids, small patterns. Closed-toe, smooth leather pumps, hosiery. Plain or cap-toe oxfords for men.	

Business Smart: Stylish and softly tailored

Key detail: Sport coat for men. Jacket or blazer for women, worn with dress slacks. Skirt optional for women.

Occasions	Message Cues	Design Details	Examples
Preliminary meetings, company meetings, general sales calls, presentations, conferences. Entertaining a client for a business lunch. Off-site training day, education.	authoritative knowledgeable efficient trustworthy friendly approachable accessible capable less formal	Unmatched suiting. Sport coat can be worn with a collar shirt or crew neck. Coordinated separates for women. Jacket/blazer with different dress slacks. Tie or no tie for men. Structured mixed with unstructured. Tasseled, plain or buckled slip-on loafers for men, slip-on closed-toe leather shoes for women.	

Business Casual: Informal

Key detail: Collared shirt for men and women, worn with dress pants and NO jacket.

Occasions	Message Cues	Design Details	Examples
Back office, preparatory meetings, projects, education. Casual Friday lunch with staff. Off-site training day.	informal relaxed creative individualistic efficient flexible cooperative artistic approachable influential conscientious knowledgeable	Coordinated separates, no jacket or jacket off. Dress shirt or blouse with collar unbuttoned at neck. Dress polo shirt with collar. Softer, curved lines and shapes mixed with some straight lines. Light, medium, dark color mix. Softer fabrics like knits, cotton blends, corduroy and silk. Slip-on, soft-sole, closed-toe leather shoe.	

Weekend Attire: Untailored

Key detail: Collarless shirt for men and women.
Not to be worn in the office unless authorized by your company.

Occasions	Message Cues	Design Details	Examples
Physical labor, off-site retreat, weekend, team-building event, blue collar.	hard working unofficial responsive easy going dependable strong efficient casual athletic	Non-suited, unstructured, durable fabrics like denim, khaki, corduroy, knits, and micro fiber. Lighter, brighter color mix. Separates not always coordinated. Active sport clothes. Boots, sandals, tennis shoes, or flats. Comfort is the key.	

I often find myself coaching clients who need to see the difference between a dress slack and a casual pant. Begin by elevating your look to another level by paying more attention to the quality of the slack. What is the difference between these two selections? The dress slack fabric and finish should hang and drape nicely, with no pills to the fabric or wrinkles of any kind. "Super 100 wools" refers to the fineness of the fibers and finish that affects the appearance and drape against the body. The casual pant differs in fabric and finish. Cotton material wrinkles more and appears stiff, so the pant does not drape; it looks worn and not polished.

Creating Your Personal Style

Knowing how to send the right message through these various looks is the key to unlocking your power image. How can you create a signature look that speaks to your own personal business style?

Style designates distinction and marks the owner as extremely confident. Tom Ford, former Gucci designer, claims that, "Style is very different from fashion. Once you find something that works, keep it." Wearing your favorite color or accessory, developing a full uniform based on comfort, shows ownership, a signature marked with style. Wearing some variation of it every day isn't boring, it's just very *you.*

If you want to make a statement and create your own signature look, keep in mind that dressing with style involves more than wearing what you like. It's not about being a fashion victim. It takes strategy, knowing how to fit your clothes, to choose appropriate fabric and color, to identify details, patterns and proportions that lengthen, slim, and direct attention to and from challenged areas. Learning how to do that, along with how you carry yourself, will give you the confidence to be a man or a woman with style.

Developing Style in the Workplace—Seven Tips to Remember

1. Style does not equal fashion.

2. Style is in the details.

3. Style is knowing when to stop. Never overdo a good thing.

4. Style reflects quality and fit.

5. Style is dressing appropriately for your body type.

6. Style is wearing clothes and colors that are best for you.

7. Style is demonstrating confidence through good posture, along with appropriate mannerisms.

When working with clients on creating their own signature look, I first ask a few questions about their personality and their clothing preferences. Are they bold and daring, elegant or refined, relaxed or energetic? I find that men usually are one of these personality styles: **Sporty Natural** usually has an athletic build, **Classic** is conservative and reserved. If a male personality exudes **Romance**, he is generally more stylish, while **Drama** suggests daring and bold tendencies, and **Creative** implies more eccentric, artistic—the glam-rocker type.

I find that women have a Natural, Classic, Romantic, Dramatic or Creative personality. A **Natural** personality likes a relaxed style; she is usually very active and fun and finds it more difficult to dress up and to wear formal clothes. The **Classic** personality is elegant and refined and tends to value quality more than quantity, style more than fashion. **Romantic** types are softer in their mannerisms, more alluring. These women prefer a flowing skirt and pretty blouse to wearing jeans. In contrast, the **Dramatic** woman is bold and sophisticated; she loves to call attention to herself through her dress, poise and confidence. And then there are the **Creative** women, who refuse to have a packaged look. They like to mix unexpected pieces and carry it all off in a spectacular manner.

Whatever your style, remember to remain within the professional boundaries of dress, but find ways to express your individuality through some of the style tips to follow.

Tips On Creating Personal Style For Men And Women

Men
Express your individuality through shirts and ties. Be bold, serious, or carefree. A man could wear the same suit every day but by changing his shirt and tie, he can have a whole new look.

Find a signature color. Color is an excellent way to break out of the monotony of white shirts. Blue, pink, yellow, purple and taupe make good choices. The button-down shirt is forever; it is the most casual of dress shirts. It looks best with a sportcoat and not with a suit. A spread collar or straight collar in broadcloth gives a suit more polish.

Shoes. Polished shoes in mint condition are a sign of a well-dressed man. On casual days, wear either a plain, tasseled or buckled loafer. For more formal events, wear a pair of cap-toe or plain lace-ups in either brown, black or cordovan leather.

Accessories. Upgrading your accessories will set you apart as a man who appreciates quality and detail. Choose a briefcase that is more supple leather in black or brown with a sleek, compact design. Leather belt with silver or gold buckle is good; match belt and shoe color. Cufflinks look very polished, and so does a linen or silk pocket square. Invest in a good watch. "The watch" is an emblem for status and efficiency in business, a sign of success.

Women
Jewelry. Less is more in business dress. You can create a signature look with:

- **A lapel pin.** Whether it's a family heirloom or a modern design, it creates a style you can claim as your own.

- **A designer scarf or strands of pearls.** Give your business suit, a silk blouse, or a cashmere sweater more punch. Female politicians in particular are becoming role models for women who want to be taken seriously. Pearl jewelry rose in sales when Nancy Pelosi and other women politicians wore pearls on C-Span.

- **Earrings.** No larger than a nickel, and nothing dangling. Pearls, encased in faux gold are classic, but keep metals compatible when mixing other pieces, such as a necklace.

Adopt a Signature Color. A power color commands attention. Pick a color and make it your own. Major companies brand themselves around a certain color.

Think Small Bag. The smaller the bag, the bigger the success. Think elegant and refined leather clutch. It will fit inside your briefcase, reduces clutter, and projects a sense of control. Don't be caught looking like a bag lady, carrying an oversized bag and also a briefcase.

Shoe Wardrobe. Shoes bring personality to the conservative business suit. The style and shine reveal intention. Are you a power player, daring or elegant? Well-designed shoes exude confidence and authority. Shoes should always be in mint condition; that is, polished, no worn-down heels. Closed-toe versus open-toe shoes: closed-toe is the business norm. Open-toe shoes during summer months are acceptable, if approved by the company.

Additional Tips for Both Men and Women

A portfolio for both men and women should be able to go from the boardroom to the podium. A slim portfolio in quality leather and minimal detail to hold the bare essentials like your speech, notepad and pen, sends a message that you are in charge and on task.

Your writing piece should reflect the importance of your words. It gives you a stylish edge and defines you as a person who is precise and pays attention to detail. Choose a pen wisely and yet keep it affordable, especially if you have a habit of leaving pens behind.

Whatever your look is, Business Dress lends itself to the classic and conservative. Your best bet is to invest in classic styles for your core wardrobe and create your individuality through your accessories.

Recently I spent time with a client who was a manager in a bank. The bank's dress code was corporate conservative, from Business Tailored to Business Smart. My client felt very confined by this look. She wanted something more fun and exciting. Once we determined her style personality, which was Dramatic, I advised her that she would still need to dress conservatively, but could express drama through her hairstyle or wardrobe color, even by her eyeglasses. After work, she of course was free to express her dramatic personality in a variety of fashionable ways. I often tell businesswomen to dress for their intelligence first, and their femininity second. If you want to be regarded as a serious professional, dress like one.

Whatever you choose to buy, especially when it comes to work clothes, ask yourself: Does this ensemble fit in with the company's image? Is it appropriate? Is it professional? If not, find something else that is.

Armed with this information, where do you begin? First, evaluate your wardrobe as to what works and what does not. Second, eliminate outdated styles and worn-out clothing. Third, establish your image and recommit yourself to your career and yourself. Executive dressing is a lifetime commitment. There will be times when you need to reinvent yourself; there are promotions, job changes, and moves to new cities. Building a wardrobe requires that you know your goals, establish a budget each season, and shop wisely, with a plan. The investment in yourself and your wardrobe can lead to a big payoff in your career.

BETH THORP, AICI CIP, CMB
Powerful Impressions

Creating a powerful impression
is a life skill—
working from the inside out

(760) 814-5132
beth@powerfulimpressions.net
www.powerfulimpressions.net

Beth is a sought-after corporate trainer, providing image, wardrobe and business etiquette services to those responsible for the perception of their organization. She is President of Powerful Impressions Inc., based in Carlsbad, California. Beth coaches clients on how to create or strengthen their image and the messages they are sending out to the world.

Beth consults on color, style analysis, strategic wardrobe planning, business etiquette, nonverbal communication, voice and diction, on-camera presence, closet audits, and personal shopping. She has been consulting and speaking to companies, groups and individuals since 1985.

Beth earned advanced certification as a Certified Image Professional through AICI, Association of Image Consultants International. She's a graduate from Ray Vogue School of Design in Fashion Merchandising. She has a degree of Master of Image, Circle of Excellence, and Certified Esthetics Training from Color Me Beautiful University. She is a member of American Society of Training and Development, and Fashion Group International.

Beth's work has been featured on The Learning Channel, Oxygen TV, KUSI TV, KDCI Headline News, FM 90.0 talk radio, and in the *San Diego Tribune*, *San Diego Business Journal, Parent* magazine, and the *North County Times*. She has written scripts for, and is featured as an expert on a variety of DVDs, and is also a book author.

Business Casual
Dressing Down with Style

By Anne Sowden, AICI CIP

Believe it or not, the two most dreaded words in the business world today have nothing to do with business, but with what to wear. Those two words are "business casual."

As we all know, business casual has been around since the 90s, when the business world embraced this new way of dressing. Company dress codes were revised, and everyone thought it was cool to dress more casually for work.

The Challenges of Business Casual

With this new way of dressing came a number of challenges.

- **Knowing what to wear for different business situations.** Before, you put on a suit, and that would carry you through every business situation. Now, you have to think about what you will be doing each day and take the time to plan what to wear.

- **What If.** No matter how much you planned, there was always the possibility of "what if." What if I get called into an important meeting? What if my biggest client drops in unexpectedly? What if they want to interview me for the evening news?

- **Being Taken Seriously.** This is particularly applicable for women. When women dress down, they lose all power and authority. One client told me that she hated business casual because she didn't look like a grownup and no one took her seriously.

- **Setting the Standard.** As an executive, your employees look to you to know what to wear. If you turn up in ripped jeans and a grubby T-shirt, then your staff will, too.

- **Casual Clothing; Casual Attitude.** With time, business casual became more casual, and so did work habits and attitudes. How do you get everyone back to business and tell them how to dress?

Business Casual Defined

In their 1999 book, *Business Casual Made Easy* (Business Casual Publications, New York), Ilene Amiel and Angie Michael described business casual as a merger of two distinctly different clothing styles, business and casual. It combines the professionalism and credibility of business clothing with the comfort and creativity of casual clothing. By using extensive research, they developed three levels of business casual—classic, smart, relaxed—based on industry and geography.

- **Classic.** One step down from traditional business clothing. The key item of clothing is a jacket. This level is typically worn in the hospitality, financial and professional services industries in major metropolitan areas.

- **Smart.** Two-piece outfits or layers. It is the most widely accepted interpretation of business casual across Canada and the U.S.

- **Relaxed.** The most casual, is recommended only for organizations that permit denim and jeans, such as IT and new media. It is sometimes adopted by organizations as a summer or Casual Friday dress code.

While the overall concept of business casual has remained the same, the three levels of business casual have evolved. Businesspeople are now dressing down by degrees and for context.

Appearance as Communication

We sometimes forget that our appearance is one of our most powerful nonverbal communications tools. We can use it to send subtle but strong messages. For example, if you are tall and always wear dark colors, you might be considered intimidating. By adding a light-color shirt or top, you will appear more approachable. Or, if you usually wear a suit with a shirt and tie, simply removing the tie and unbuttoning your shirt (one or two buttons) will make you appear more open, or less buttoned-up.

When dressing for work, think of the message you want your appearance to send. If you want to come across as powerful and authoritative, wear dark colors and smooth fabrics. If you have a tough message to tell your employees, wear muted colors and softer fabrics.

Easy Ways to Make an Outfit More Casual

Color. Adding color is one of the easiest ways to make an outfit more casual. Combine neutral colors such as navy, gray, brown, taupe and black with non-traditional colors such as blue, red, yellow, burgundy, orange, pink and turquoise. If you normally wear a dark suit with a white or pale blue shirt, try a deeper-colored shirt that complements your coloring. For women, pants with a matched or unmatched jacket, and a bright colored sweater or top, create a casual, professional look.

Pattern. When I say "pattern," clients often panic. Men will tell me "I don't do pattern," while wearing a striped tie. Women cringe and say, "I don't do flowers." While stripes and flowers are patterns, there are also checks, herringbone, paisley, abstract prints, polka dots. And yes, adding pattern can be scary but it is also very easy. Adding just one pattern can make something more casual. Simply wearing a striped shirt or a checked jacket adds pattern.

Texture. How a fabric looks and feels. Typically, a smooth, stiff fabric such as wool is considered formal when used in suits. Fabrics such as tweeds, knits, corduroy, and sweaters are often soft to the touch and can instantly make any outfit more casual. Try a tweed jacket with a pair of wool gabardine pants. Or instead of a shirt under a suit, women can wear a sweater or knit top.

Accessories. Shoes, jewelry, bags, belts and scarves are a quick and easy way to make an outfit more casual. Metals, gemstones, gold and pearls are formal. Jewelry made from items such as wood, plastic, silver and ethnic motifs are more casual. For women, an ethnic style necklace or belt worn with a formal suit instantly adds a less formal tone. Similarly, a patterned scarf also adds instant informality. Shoes, too, can add informality. As a guideline, thin-soled shoes are considered dressy, while thicker soles are more casual. For women, a lower-heeled shoe or boot automatically makes your look more casual.

Taking the Fear Out of Dressing Down: A Case History

Bill had recently changed jobs. A seasoned customer service manager in a bank, he moved to a more senior role with an IT company. As expected, Bill made the transition quickly, adapting readily to the entrepreneurial culture and learning new buzzwords so he could communicate with his staff. He thought things were going really well until he had his three-month review. The president explained that Bill's staff thought he was unfriendly and remote because he always wore a suit. To help make the transition from formal to less formal clothing, the president asked me to work with Bill.

The first step was to look at Bill's wardrobe. He had two types of clothing: formal—suits, and really casual—jeans and sweatshirts. Bill's suits were all dark colors—grey, navy and black. His dress shirts were white or pale blue and his ties had conservative stripes. Clearly, he needed to add some color and variety. With color analysis, we determined that soft muted blues, grays and taupes were the most flattering for his coloring. While Bill felt comfortable with the colors, he was concerned about incorporating color into his daily routine.

We started slowly, by adding some striped shirts to his wardrobe. He wore these open at the neck with his suits. To get comfortable with the look, I encouraged him to walk around the office and have staff meetings without a jacket.

Then we moved him from suits into sports jackets and coordinating pants. I suggested he try a sports jacket a couple of days a week. Once he was comfortable with that look, we added more sports jackets, coordinating pants, shirts, ties and sweaters. We worked together to develop different looks—mixing and matching colors, adding textures and layers. I reorganized his closet, took photos and prepared wardrobe charts so that getting ready in the morning was as easy as putting on a suit. In addition to clothing, we picked out new eyeglass frames and visited a hairstylist for a more modern cut.

Bill's transformation from buttoned-up to open and friendly was quite a journey. His staff now finds him approachable. They compliment him on his clothing and ask him where he shops. Some have even asked for lessons on mixing and matching colors. The president says he looks like a new man!

Looking Professional in Every Situation: A Case History

As president of a manufacturing company, Lindsay meets with suppliers and distributors, and attends trade shows and industry functions. After a recent strategic planning retreat, her company realized that they needed to re-brand to attract new customers. This would mean travel throughout North America and Europe to meet industry leaders, potential suppliers and distributors and to attend trade shows.

Lindsay's style of dressing hasn't changed throughout her career. She started working in the plant, became a supervisor, and moved up through management to become president. Most days, she wears jeans with sweaters. For tradeshows and industry functions, she has one black suit that she bought about ten years ago. She wears her hair in a ponytail and is uncomfortable with makeup.

To work with Lindsay, I really needed to understand what she did every day, so I shadowed her. We talked about her vision, her long-term and short-term objectives for the company, and her travel plans. Then we focused on her vision for herself. She knew she needed to look more polished and professional, but was afraid she would lose her "self" in the process.

It was quite an education. I assessed her colors, helped her understand her body shape and how to enhance it, introduced her to different clothing styles, presented her with options, and sent her to a hairstylist and makeup artist. In addition, I coached Lindsay on international business and social etiquette.

To build her wardrobe, I created capsules of basic clothing items such as pants, tops, jackets and accessories that worked together. See more on capsule dressing in Karen Brunger's chapter, *Capsule Dressing for Men and Women,* on page 35. I picked simple, classic styles that could go from the shop floor to the boardroom, after a quick stop to remove the hardhat. I picked a combination of fabrics—wool with a bit of Lycra for ease of movement, washable microfiber for travel and plant visits, and cotton for comfort. We replaced Lindsay's black suit with interesting jackets—tweed, tone on tone, fitted dark-wash denim, plain with a trim that said "professional" yet reflected her down-to-earth style and personality. Rather than shirts, I selected tops and sweaters in soft colors and subtle patterns.

After her first business trip to Europe, Lindsay and I met to debrief. She said there were a couple of companies interested in distribution deals, so the trip was worthwhile. More importantly, Lindsay felt her updated image really reflected who she was and helped her represent her company with confidence and professionalism.

Seven Ways to Keep It Stylish

We all know that we have to keep our business skills up-to-date, but we're so busy doing that, we forget we need to keep our wardrobe up-to-date. It doesn't need to take a lot of time, but even the slightest update can make a big difference in how you are perceived.

1. **Add one or two items each season.** I know you buy classics and they should last forever. But eventually they go out of style or wear out and need to be replaced every few years. Add a new jacket or pair of pants that mixes and matches with what you already have.

2. **Buy a shirt, tie, blouse, sweater or top in one of the season's hottest colors.** This is an easy way to make an old outfit look brand new. If you normally wear a solid-color shirt with your sports jacket, try a striped one. Remember to check that the color is flattering; otherwise, you'll have a lot of people inquiring about your health.

3. **Add new accessories.** A new belt, shoes, jewelry, scarf, watch or bag can make an outfit look completely different. Think about replacing your diving watch with something more streamlined. Add a chunky necklace. Retire those shoes that used to be black but have turned grey. Subliminally you're saying, "I'm on top of my game."

4. **Eyeglass frames.** This is one of the quickest ways to update your look. Get a new style every couple of years when you get your eyes checked. Those aviator frames you've been wearing for years may be back in style, but even Tom Cruise has moved on.

5. **Update your makeup.** Like clothing, makeup lines bring in different looks and colors each season. While the look may not suit you, try a fresh color of lipstick, eyeliner or shadow. If you paint your nails, try one of the new nail colors.

6. **Get a new hairstyle, or change the color of your hair.** After new glasses, a new hairstyle is an instant way to change your look. It can make you look and feel like a million bucks. If you're not sure about a new hair color, try a semi-permanent hair

color that will wash out. Remember, though, coloring your hair is a commitment and you have to keep it up.

7. Shop in your closet. We're all guilty of the 80/20 rule— wearing twenty percent of our wardrobe eighty percent of the time. So what about that 80 percent you don't wear? Get an image consultant to help you find new ways to wear things. It's amazing what a fresh pair of eyes can do for your wardrobe.

When getting ready for work, there is really only one thing to ask yourself. What message do I want my appearance to send? Take the time to regularly assess your wardrobe. Use the guidelines in this chapter to update, refine or redefine your look so it always says what you want it to say. If you think of your appearance as a communications tool like your computer or cell phone, you'll never have to worry about business casual again. You'll always send the right message.

ANNE SOWDEN, AICI CIP
Here's Looking at You

Inspiring confidence and trust

(416) 429-8028
anne@hereslookingatyou.ca
www.hereslookingatyou.ca

An effective image makes the difference between inspiring confidence, building your own confidence or losing trust. Anne understands the issues and challenges facing business. Before launching Here's Looking at You, she gained extensive national and international marketing and communications experience in both the public and private sectors. She combines that business expertise with image consulting and training in adult learning to help organizations improve their image.

Through workshops and seminars, Anne provides image enhancement advice, verbal and nonverbal communication skills education, culture-specific coaching and etiquette and protocol training. She works with teams to develop dress codes, improve social interaction skills and refine their business image so they represent your company with confidence and professionalism. Her clients come from business sectors such as financial services, information technology, pharmaceutical, retail, real estate, energy, education and not-for-profit.

Known for her approachability and practicality, Anne also works one-on-one with clients in various ways, including assessing their wardrobes, taking them shopping, helping with verbal and nonverbal communication, or reviewing business and social etiquette. Her clients gain confidence from an enhanced image that strengthens their authenticity.

Anne is a Certified Professional Member of the Association of Image Consultants International and is a past president of the Canada/ Toronto chapter.

Be Critical of Your Clothes, Not Your Body
Choosing What's Right for Your Body Type

By Jennifer Bressie

Many people believe if they spend a lot of money on clothes, they will look fantastic all the time. Here's some very important information: if you don't buy clothes to fit your particular shape, you won't look as great! Even if you spend a fortune on designer labels, the most important piece of the getting-dressed puzzle is making sure the clothes you wear fit your body properly. Are the sleeves long enough? Does the fabric pucker anywhere? Does it make you look larger than you are? These are all common mistakes I see when working with clients.

Besides basic grooming, such as brushing our teeth and combing our hair, getting dressed is one of the few things we must do, or should do, every day. Shouldn't it be fun? Wouldn't it be great to enjoy it, even love it? I know I do, which is why I'm always surprised when I meet people who don't. In fact, for many of my new clients, getting dressed makes them miserable. Why? Because their closet is a mess, or because they've recently put on weight or lost weight. Whatever the reason, they hate it!

You might hate it too, and that's okay. Here's what I want you to know: it is to your advantage to take the time to understand clothing and your particular body. Through this knowledge, you can stop blaming your body for not being perfect and start accepting your beautiful body for the wonder it is. Hopefully you will even love, celebrate and be grateful for your body.

Find the Right Size—Ignore The Numbers

When I first met my client Sara, a management consultant, the main frustration she expressed was how hard it was for her to find items she liked that also fit her body properly. The same was true for her husband, Peter, a chief financial officer. Both of them had become so tired of trying on clothes, only to leave the mall empty-handed, again and again.

What were they doing wrong? First, they assumed that clothes should fit them off the rack—with no alterations. They were also clinging to some old sizes that no longer reflected their current bodies. Sara's body had changed with her pregnancies. As hard as it may be, you must ignore the size on the tag and focus on the fit! Why? Because each manufacturer utilizes a different fit model to design its clothes. The result is that the same size from different manufacturers can be completely different.

If you can't find a perfect fit off the racks, purchase clothing that fits the largest part of your body. For example, my hips require a larger pant size than my waist. I buy pants to fit my hips, and have the waist taken in. Same thing with jackets; my shoulders are broad, but jackets that fit my shoulders tend to be too large elsewhere. So I have them taken in where they are too big.

Shop by fit, not by size. And remember, the tailor is your friend. If you do not have a good tailor, note that many department stores have tailors on staff. They can be called into the dressing room when you try on an item.

Be sure to have a chat with your tailor before he or she takes a pair of scissors to your new designer suit. A good tailor will tell you the types of alterations possible in any given garment. In general, sleeve length and pant length, waist in or out—no more than an inch or so—are examples of tailoring that are pretty straightforward.

Once we got Sara and Peter fitted in the correct size and had some simple alterations done, they were happy dressers.

Be Comfortable

In addition to looking good, a proper fit usually means that you are comfortable. If some part of your body is popping out, chances are you are not very comfortable. And I don't just mean physical comfort—mental comfort is important too. So spend some time in front of the mirror, taking stock of what you've got and what you feel good about showing. Maybe you have great arms, or beautiful eyes, or fantastic calves. If you love your arms, find some super short-sleeved, sleeveless or sheer-sleeved blouses. Wear your eye color in a sweater or shirt to call attention to your eyes. If you have great legs, find a lovely knee-length skirt. This logic, of course, stops with the abs. If you've got a six-pack, super for you, but please save it for the beach. There is nothing worse than inappropriate attire in a professional setting. See Colleen Abrie's chapter, *Head to Toe: Details Matter*, on page 85 about the details. They count!

Know Your Body Type

Everyone knows that bodies come in all shapes and sizes. What everyone doesn't know, however, is that there are different ways to flatter, and camouflage, the various body shapes. Some bodies require soft, flowing fabrics; others need a little more structure. Some bodies need belts; some need to avoid belts.

By the way, please do not judge your body type and wish you had another. You've got what you've got, and it's not going to change. It isn't a function of weight or working out. Sure that can help you look and feel your best, but your basic body shape is what it is. You just need to know which one it is, and what to do with it to always look your best.

There are dozens of ways to classify body shapes. Some theories classify everyone as a type of fruit (apples, pears). Some utilize a line and curve format (square, circle). I find most helpful the six body types that Carla Mason Mathis and Helen Villa Connor share in their book *The Triumph of Individual Style* (1994, Timeless Edition)

See the chart on page 79. These six types—Rectangle, Oval, Hourglass, Figure Eight, Triangle and Inverted Triangle—are easy to identify without a lot of measuring and fuss.

To quickly assess your body type, stand in front of a full-length mirror with no clothes on and squint. What is your silhouette? Are you long-waisted, short-waisted or proportionate? You can tell this by placing your hands at your natural waist. Are they closer to your head or your feet? For most people, it's not noticeably either.

Long-Waisted Versus Short-Waisted

If your waist is closer to your toes than the top of your head, you are long-waisted. Your pants should be hemmed to the floor to give the illusion of length and balance. Women can wear a high-heeled shoe and have the hem of the pants extended to the floor, which literally adds length to your legs.

If your waist is closer to your head, you are short-waisted. You can create the illusion of a longer, proportionate silhouette by wearing belts at the hip or wearing fitted tops, untucked.

Chart Note: Men will most likely remain in the rectangle, oval, triangle and inverted triangle shapes.

After you have decided if you are long-waisted or short-waisted, go ahead and measure your shoulders, waist and hips to determine your shape. Are those measurements within a couple of inches of one another? If you are really having trouble, you may want to consider hiring a professional. Many image consultants perform body type analysis as part of their service offering.

Rectangle

Characteristics: Shoulders and hips symmetrical. Waist is also this same size, with minimal indent.

Shopping Tips for Women:

- Boat neck and scoop neck tops draw the eye upward
- A-line tops create curves at the waist
- Sheath dresses or wrap dresses
- Pants: straight or boot-cut to suggest curves

Shopping Tips for Men:

- Often rectangle men are quite tall; if so, best to avoid pin-striped suits
- If not tall, a pin-striped suit would look great!

Oval

Characteristics: Shoulders and hips roughly same size. Waist or middle is wider.

Shopping Tips for Women:

- Tops should be v-necks or wide scoop necks; military-style jackets add volume to shoulder area. Choose puff sleeves or flutter sleeves to add volume up top.
- Dresses should have off the shoulder or sweetheart necklines. Empire dresses to add bulk on top and skim over body.
- Flared or fluted hems, do not tuck in tops, no belts.

Shopping Tips for Men:

- Wear single column of color underneath coordinating jacket
- Jackets with vertical striping at shoulder or bulky details at shoulder
- Sweaters with leather or suede at shoulder area with V or zipper front

Hourglass

Characteristics: Shoulders and hips roughly same size, squared. Waist is narrower.

Shopping Tips for Women:
• Desirable! Show it off, no balloon tops or dresses
• Nothing that hangs straight from your bust
• Use belts if you are not too short-waisted *(see note)*

Figure Eight

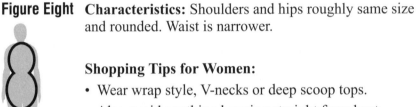

Characteristics: Shoulders and hips roughly same size and rounded. Waist is narrower.

Shopping Tips for Women:
• Wear wrap style, V-necks or deep scoop tops.
• Also avoid anything hanging straight from bust
• Wrap style, fitted sheath dresses
• Stovepipe or straight-leg pants
• Use belts if you are not too short-waisted *(see note)*

Triangle

Characteristics: Shoulders narrower than hips

Two types: Waist is narrow like shoulders or waist is full like hips

Shopping Tips for Women:
• Balance top and bottom, shoulder pads or epaulets on jackets
• Wide collars or horizontal lines at the shoulder area
• On bottom, wear darker colors; wear body-skimming fabrics
• Straight-legged pants, gored or trumpet skirts, all hemmed at the narrowest part of leg

Shopping Tips for Men:
• See above tips for jackets and shirts
• Shirts should be untucked, structure at shoulder
• Sweaters with bulk at shoulder and should skim the body

Inverted Triangle

Characteristics: Shoulders wider than hips and waist

Shopping Tips for Women:
- Wear fuller skirts or fuller-legged pants to create the illusion of balance

Shopping Tips for Men:
- Considered very desirable, wear shirts tucked in
- Wear straight-legged pants
- This is the only male body type that can wear a double-breasted blazer well and it should be tailored correctly so it doesn't gap open when buttoned

General Flattering Tips for All Body Types

For women, a V-neck or scoop neck is universally flattering. It draws attention to the center of your body, especially if you happen to be wearing a fantastic necklace.

For men, always fit your pants to your natural waist. Men often gain weight in the stomach area, which under no circumstances should hang over your pants. Pants should not fit too tightly, as you should have room to breathe and sit comfortably. If you have recently lost weight in this area, spend a few dollars to have the waists of your pants taken in.

An ideal fit for both sexes follows your natural body silhouette closely. It does not cling. In general, if there are wrinkles in the fabric, the garment is either too big or too small. In either case, this only makes the wearer look larger. If the item is too large and the wearer is buried under all that fabric, the end result is that visually, you are that size. If the item is too small, the eye is drawn to the areas in which it is too tight. It's like a highlighter pen on the flaws of your body; no one wants that.

Prints, patterns, accessories and details must be in proportion to your body. For example, a large, muscular man wearing a tiny printed polka dot shirt looks out of proportion. Likewise, a tiny woman carrying a purse that she herself could fit into also looks out of proportion.

The process of learning how to understand your body and how to flatter it is a remarkable journey, and the destination is self-acceptance and more fun getting dressed. But the journey also requires trying on lots of clothes, which can be time-consuming. So if you find yourself frustrated, you may want to enlist the services of an image professional.

Case in point: I have spent several months with a client, Janette, a director of a large non-profit organization. We performed a full body analysis. We shopped numerous times together and she has tried on many items that have worked—and many that have not. It's been a long process, but over time she has learned how to highlight her assets and camouflage other areas, and I have watched her become more confident, more adventurous in her style selections, and ultimately more joyful about getting dressed. I wish that for everyone!

While learning to dress your body shape properly takes time, it also means accepting that there is nothing wrong with your body. You just need to be trained in how to work with it. It can be challenging, but the results are life-changing.

By putting attention on your shape and fit, my hope is that you will start being kinder to yourself and more critical of the clothes you purchase. Enjoy the process to creating the most flattering you!

JENNIFER BRESSIE
Image and Style Consultant

Bring the joy back into getting dressed!

(650)867-5399
jennifer@shoppersf.com
www.shoppersf.com

Jennifer Bressie is an experienced image consultant based in the San Francisco Bay Area. With over twenty years of expertise in fashion, she is known for her ability to guide her clients through the development of their personal style. A dedicated closet-clutter eliminator who believes that getting dressed should be fun, she is committed to assisting her clients to achieve that joy.

Jennifer serves a diverse group of clients, including women, men, teens and children. She works with both individuals and groups. Privately, she assists her clients with body and style analysis, closet audits, and personal shopping. She is known to be helpful with gift giving as well! With groups she has presented talks on various aspects of image, including accessory selection, style definition and closet clearing. Jennifer looks for fun and joy in all that she tackles. She brings this joyful spirit to working with her clients.

Jennifer is an Associate Member of CDI (Colour Designers International) and is an active member of AICI. Currently she is serving as the Secretary of the AICI SF Bay Area Chapter.

Head to Toe
Details Matter

By Colleen Abrie, AICI FLC, CDI

Don't you love to people-watch? The mall, the airport, bars and restaurants, and of course our favorite outdoor café or coffee shop—all offer a visual feast to see how people put themselves together.

And yet when I discuss how important image details are with clients, some will argue that details don't matter. Why, then, do we find ourselves critiquing how others look? Why are we sometimes offended by the very presence of a particular person?

Consider this: what if you called for help from a police officer and he showed up with shaggy, long hair, reeking of cologne, buttons missing from his uniform, his shoes, belt and holster looking like they had been through a tornado? This picture is extreme, but my point is, how safe you would feel?

Details are one of those subconscious communicators that people don't realize are deal-breakers. These subtle infractions may make others be polite to your face but talk about you behind your back, or worse, not take you seriously.

When things are not up to culturally acceptable standards, for example, in the professional business arena, we are unable to focus on critical issues during our interaction with others. This can impair our effectiveness in being productive, reaching our goals, and experiencing the personal satisfaction of a job well done. These are topics that could potentially create a barrier between one's current position and advancement in business and relationships.

Think about it—when things are visually in order, there is a certain stillness of the mind. We don't even notice when things look right because we can tend to the matter at hand without distractions.

Creating new habits that champion a well-trained eye for details will provide powerful results in your personal and professional life. Let's review some of the basics that can create roadblocks to our success.

Wardrobe Commandments to Follow Every Day

- **Pledge thy commitment.** Thou shalt not show or draw attention to erogenous body parts, tattoos, or underarms in a professional work environment.
- **Sleeveless tops with flabby arms** are never a good choice for business. Style message: "I don't consider my shortcomings."
- **Waist and tummy peek-a-boos** offer too much information. Style message: "Don't take me seriously; this is just a job."
- **Thong or panty-peek-a-boos** are crimes against humanity. Style message: "I'm unconcerned with my effect on you."
- **Too much cleavage.** Style message: "If this was not for sale, why is this being advertised?"
- **Short skirts.** Style message: "Watch out, she's a man-eater . . ." Too sexy and too distracting for the office.
- **Uneven skin quality on your thighs and fanny.** Style message: "My life is a bumpy road." This skin problem shows under many garments that are too lightweight, unlined, or light in color. Get a small hand mirror for a clear rear view. No matter your size, shapers can smooth the road to success.

- **Panty-lines.** Shockingly, this is a global infraction that occurs every day of the week. Style message: "Stare at my backside and forget everything I just said." Donna Karan's waistband-free smoothers can eliminate the problem.

- **Wearing garments with food, oil, or coffee stains.** Take the garment to a drycleaner, or put it out to pasture. Style message: "I'm messy," or, "I do things haphazardly."

- **Pet hair on clothing.** Very distracting and brings up issues of attention to sanitation and carelessness. Style message: "I am not conscientious."

Garment Fit = Ready, Set, Go

Garment fit is crucial, because when your clothes work with your body, you're ready for anything. A good fit equals comfort and confidence, and is flattering no matter the size or shape of your body.

- **Falling apart at the seams.** Ripped seams say your garment is either too small or it's tired.
- **Bumpy zippers.** You know—the ripply, snake-like zipper line on certain fabrics? Good advice says toss it, or don't buy it, because it can't be fixed.
- **Scruffy hems on slacks, jeans, and wrists.** They look like they've been dragged for miles. Style message: "I'm dragging myself through life."
- **Holey or torn fabrics.** These are best worn at home while cleaning the garage or doing your best version of rock-'n'-roll air guitar.
- **Underarm stains or fading color.** This says, "I'm tarnished," "I'm all washed up."
- **Missing buttons.** They say, "I've lost control and I'm clueless because I'm still wearing this garment."

- **Button-blouse bra peek-a-boo.** This says, "I'm busting out of here!" Go to www.bugcatcherz.com and order, No See'ems®, an invisible solution.

- **Tugging at bra straps, waistbands or undergarments.** This says, "I'm trying to pull it together but obviously, I'm not there yet." Adjust your bra straps when needed. Avoid wearing waistbands that are too low or too loose. Try seamless undergarments from: www.nononsense.com.

- **Fabric snags.** This says, "I'm all hung up." Order a Dritz® Snag Nab-it from www.joann.com.

- **Pilling on knits.** Have you ever heard of the term cliffhanger? Get your fabric shaver at www.evercare.com or www.oreck.com.

Hot Tip. Make a closet 911 kit with fashion tape, safety pins, a seam ripper, sewing kit, a lint roller and a fabric shaver with extra batteries. Keep it handy where you relax and watch TV or listen to music and multitask during these hours. You'll see how easy it is to keep up.

Size Matters

- **Garments that are too big.** They say, "I'm drowning."Skirt and pant hemlines that are too long. Style message: "I've been cut off at the knees."

- **Garments that are too tight at the hip and crotch.** They make cat whiskers from fabric that is strained into horizontal pleat formations. Style message: "I'm packing in everything I can." Worse yet, vertical pulling at the end of the crotch is a neon sign that in turn, will embarrass all those who inadvertently realized they noticed. Please ditch those pants!

- **Trouser hems that are too short.** Style message: "Where's the flood?," "I don't have a clue." Crop them or toss them.

Hot Tip. Budget alterations into your clothing allowance. Don't force yourself into ready-to-wear garments or items that used to work but no longer fit. Find a reputable professional in your area by personal referral, or visit www.yelp.com.

Spot-On Accessory Statements

- **Overstuffed handbags.** They say, "I'm overloaded."

- **Scuffed and beat-up handbags or briefcases.** They say, "I'm tired and worn-out."

- **Scuffed shoes and belts.** They say, "I'm tired," or "I can't afford anything else."

- **Hosiery and leggings for conservative business should not include black or colored fishnets, or bold patterned tights, colored tights or shiny hose.** These choices are best worn after 5 p.m.

- **If you're wearing socks with trousers, buy smart.** Good-quality socks and hosiery last longer and make a successful statement.

- **Men—your socks should match your trousers.** Leave the athletic socks for the gym. What to wear with your blue jeans? Match your shoes or wear blue socks.

- **Jewelry overkill.** This is wearing every ring you own at the same time with a necklace, dangle earrings, a bracelet, and a timepiece. Style message: "I have too much going on to be effective."

Hot Tip. If your outfit is simple, choose one or two accessories to be your focal point. This brings drama and power into your overall appearance. If your outfit has a "star" piece, maybe an unusual jacket, one simple accessory such as earrings will finish the look without competing with the jacket.

- **Brooch placement.** Most women place a brooch a few inches above their breast. This draws the eye down from your face and makes you look tired because of unflattering facial lines.

Hot Tip. Place your hand on your heart as if you were going to pledge allegiance to the flag. At the tip of your fingers is just about the right place to pin your brooch—on either side of your body. This draws the eye upward toward your face while drawing the eye away from your bustline.

Avoid Fabric Fiascos

This is one of those grey areas in wardrobe planning that confuses people, and so they often send a mixed message. For example, if you live in a tropical location, wearing linen in January is perfectly acceptable. If you live in a climate where it's winter in January, you must put aside linen clothes until the true launch of spring. Style message: "I'm unsophisticated."

- **Mixed-up fabrics.** Linen fabrics should never be combined with fall or winter fabrics. Winter fabrics are wool, cashmere, leather or synthetic blends. Acceptable combinations are silk, chiffon, cotton, or other sheer, matte, lightweight fabrics, knits and denim.
- **Wearing fabrics together that cause a "riding up" effect.** There's nothing worse than putting on a jacket with a completed outfit that produces a war between the fabric naps. Style message: "I'm inexperienced."
- **Combining light and dark fabrics that leave traces on each other.** Much like pet hair, if you're wearing pieces together that shed residual fibers you look like you've lounged with a litter of kitties. Style message: "I'm unaware."
- **Clingy or slinky fabrics should not be worn for conservative business.** An exception, for business casual, could be those fabrics worn on super-fit bodies with small bustlines. But beware, it still draws attention to your body and others may not hear all you have to say because they're focused on your form.

- **Mixing patterns can be modern and current.** However, done poorly, it sends a message of haphazard thinking or being out-of-touch. My best advice is to avoid experiments and hire an image consultant.

- **Faded denim jeans on a grown-up woman are outdated and out of touch.** Dark denim is much more flattering and more appropriate for certain business casual arenas.

- **Men wearing denim.** The main focus should be on a good fit. Denim is tough, so guys can wear jeans for years before replacing them. Are your jeans long enough for a soft break at the front? Long enough at the back to be an inch above your heel? Is your waistband at your navel and not below your stomach? If not, get a new pair.

- **Leather pants or skirts are not for conservative business wear.** They are a better choice for business casual, combined simply with an elegant sweater or silk blouse.

Give Attention to Your Grooming

Neglected grooming habits speak to a lack of self-care and self-esteem. Grooming is the most disagreeable offense to encounter because oftentimes, it is truly offensive to the visual and olfactory senses. The worst grooming offenses are:

Bad Breath. Don't count on anyone telling you that you need freshening. Keeping sugar-free mints on hand is your best protection.

- **Halitosis can be a chronic condition.** Unless you live and work on an island, take action and see your doctor.

- **People who have poor dental hygiene or don't eat regular meals.** Those on a diet, who love spicy foods, or who don't drink enough water can also have halitosis. Smokers have a double whammy. Lots of mints and hand-washing are your best antidotes.

Gum-chewing is not acceptable in business and will diminish your credibility.

Body Odor. If you are challenged, replace your tops and shirts regularly, because once that odor gets into the fibers, it's never coming out. Your body heat will reactivate the odor—even on freshly cleaned clothing. Synthetic fibers are the worst offenders. These need to be replaced more often than natural-fiber garments.

Fragrance. Overkill fragrance is noxious, no matter how expensive. Once you get used to your own fragrance, you can't smell it any more. Remember—fragrance is not meant to cover up smoking habits or body odor.

Stained Teeth. The "million-dollar smile" doesn't have to mean perfect teeth. With a minimal investment, whiter teeth will take years off your age and will make wearing white more becoming. Always check your teeth after eating!

Dirty Eyeglasses. Dirty eyewear says "Nutty Professor" or "Mrs. Magoo." Get in the habit of cleaning your eyeglasses daily before you leave for the office.

Facial Hair. Unruly eyebrows, sideburns, lip, chin, and nose hair. Just because you can't see it doesn't mean it's not there. Magnifying mirrors offer a world of clarity. A trusted beauty professional can clean up your act with regular visits, and give you peace of mind when natural light catches your face.

Makeup—Make it Simple.

- **Too much eyeshadow.** This can shrink your eyes into your head and give you the impression of being harsh or mean.
- **Overly bright lip colors for the office.** These are overdone and a bit tart.
- **Contrasting lip liner.** This screams "1980s discothèque."

- **A foundation color line between your face and neck.** This makes you look like you applied spackle. The color tone of your neck and décolleté should be considered when selecting a foundation color. Having your foundation application align with your natural skin quality creates a look that is fresh and beautiful. Treat yourself and get a beauty update.

Skin Care

Your skin is one of the first things people will notice about you when something is amiss. Do not overlook this important area. If you have acne, flaky skin or rosacea, work with a skin professional to do all that you can, stay on track, and it will get better. If you're not working with a skin professional, just remember that people can't hear your message, since their focus is on your skin. Wouldn't you rather have their confidence and not their sympathy?

Hair—Your Crowning Glory

There is nothing worse than a bad hair day that goes on repeatedly. Make a commitment to yourself and find a stylist and a home-care system that works for your lifestyle.

- **Hair color roots.** Bad news. Roots always look cheap, and are aging. Keep your appointments at all cost.

- **Oily, lifeless, shaggy, grown-out hair.** It says, "I'm unworthy, don't bother." Stay on track with a good stylist who gives you a lift every six weeks.

- **Frizzy or out-of-control hair.** It says, "I'm uncooperative." The right product regime can tame your tresses.

- **Dandruff.** Brush your hair vigorously before you shower and use treatment shampoo during every wash. Live with a lint roller in every corner of your life.

Remember Your Hands and Feet

- **Chipped polish appears shoddy.** Polishing your nails is a commitment. If you can't keep up, buy single-use packets of polish remover for your handbag or tote. Visit www.drugstore.com.
- **Dirt under fingernails.** This says, "Grubby."
- **Neon nail colors, decals, nail art and vamp polish.** These are for after hours.
- **Excessively dry hands, untended cuticles and crusty heels are reptilian.** All are to be avoided.

I suggest you review this chapter with a trusted friend. Take a hard look at your clothing, accessories and personal habits. Ask yourself if your clothing and the way you put yourself together tells the story of where you are going rather than where you have been.

Every successful professional has a team of experts for every special need in their life. Do you need a quality stylist, tailor or esthetician? Pick up your laptop and get started finding them now.

Using the secrets of head-to-toe details, you will have so many ways to highlight and refine your image. Then you can get down to business, be part of the team, take center stage, negotiate, win, have more fun, more freedom, and finally, take charge of your future.

COLLEEN ABRIE, AICI FLC, CDI
Head-to-Toe Personal Stylist

(408) 772-3358
colleen@colleenabrie.com
www.colleenabrie.com

Colleen Abrie's exceptional skills as a professional hair stylist and make-up artist are expertly blended with a head-to-toe focus on total image. Her personal style strategies with defining detail offer powerful results for men and women.

With a sharp and experienced eye, Colleen works with clients to create a dynamic image no matter their size, age or budget. Colleen shares her expertise through fun, positive communication in an educational service relationship. Colleen's specialties include: head-to-toe preparation for photo shoots and special events, closet audit and organization, figure and style analysis, personal shopping, custom clothing and jewelry design, wardrobe coordination for travel and packing, and eyewear and accessory selection.

Colleen's dynamic speaking and presenting style has landed her engagements such as fashion commentator for plus-size women's fashion at Saks Fifth Avenue, San Francisco. She has coordinated and presented multiple fashion trend shows with Saks Fifth Avenue, Bloomingdale's, Emporio Armani, Judith Ripka, and other San Francisco Bay Area vendors.

Colleen is a past president and member of the Association of Image Consultants International, San Francisco Bay Area Chapter. She is also past president of, and certified as a Color Expert for Colour Designers International, the Bay Area training organization for color analysis and appearance education.

Closet R$_x$:
Your Prescription
for an Ailing Closet
How to Make Your Wardrobe Well

By Divya Vashi

Are you like many people who say they have a closet full of clothes but nothing to wear? Do you have difficulty finding what you need immediately in your closet? Do you have too many clothes and too little space? Does news of an upcoming important meeting make you plan your next shopping trip?

Having a closet in chaos is a common challenge. You certainly were not taught about this subject in business school. Still, having a place for your clothes and knowing how to take good care of them is an essential part of maintaining a healthy wardrobe. Think about it—you care for your body with a good diet, enough sleep, water and exercise, so why not care for the clothes you put on your body?

Picture this: You are running late for work. It is a big day, and you want to look your best and make a good impression. You open your closet and get snowed under by a pile of clothes. Remember how you haphazardly threw everything into the closet last evening before going to the movies?

You find the jacket, but the pants are missing. They are in there, somewhere, you know, but where? Your perfect outfit is lost in a perfect mess. You finally find the pants, but there is no way you can wear them. Not only are they badly wrinkled, but there are tell-tale signs of that sumptuous dinner you gorged on last weekend. How you wish your closet was not a disaster!

People like to call me a wardrobe consultant. I prefer to call myself a wardrobe doctor. I did not grow up in the most organized household, but observing my surroundings made me decide early in life that I would be organized and help others become organized. When I was in high school, I once stayed over at a friend's home and had an experience that left a lasting impression on me.

In the morning, I was awakened by panicky cries of my friend's father as he was getting ready to leave for work. "Where is my brown belt?" "Has anyone seen my new cufflinks?" "I cannot find a matching pair of socks!" Voices gradually grew louder and angrier as her parents quibbled over whose fault it was. My friend was embarrassed and confided to me that, due to her parents' busy lives, they had no time to organize anything. I was shocked when I saw her closet—it too looked like a mini tornado zone. It took us one full day to organize her closet, but the result was extremely satisfying.

When I assist my clients with their shopping needs, I first ask them to show me their closet. More often than not, we find ourselves shopping in the closet itself! Most of my clients walk away from that experience amazed at how much time, money and energy they saved in the long run.

Each of us is very busy, and most of us accept living with a disorganized and inefficient closet until we can find the day to work on it. Yet we put the task off, believing that while the closet can wait another weekend, other things on our to-do list cannot. We also secretly hope that our closet will magically "fix itself." Nobody likes a disorganized wardrobe but, given our time constraints, we tend to ignore this very important matter.

Do Not Let Clutter Control Your Life

A disorganized closet can take a toll on your mental peace in more ways than one. First, if you never find what you looking for, you have wasted precious time trying to find it, and you are left feeling exasperated. Even if you decide to leave the room for the moment, the thought of the chaos stays with you all day long, destroying your serenity.

Six Reasons to Take the Time to Take Care of Your Closet

1. Have more time; be able to get dressed in ten minutes or less.

2. Be able to create more options; mix and match your favorites

3. Accessorize better; no trouble finding matching pieces.

4. Know what you need and be able to better shop for your wardrobe.

5. Easily find your clothes in the closet because everything has its place.

6. Look better and be a happier you!

Get Ready to Get Started

The question is, where to begin? If your closet looks like "mission impossible," do not panic. You can do it, and I will show you how.

Make sure you have done the laundry recently, so that all your clothes are accessible. Take everything out of the closet. Return wire hangers to the dry cleaner. Get different types of hangers for different garments. Use cascading hangers if you do not have enough space. Avoid using clamp hangers for trousers, as they can leave marks on the fabric.

Remember not to work when you are hungry, and stay hydrated. Put your favorite music on in the background. Here are a few other things you will need to diagnose and treat your ailing closet:

- Plenty of uninterrupted time
- A few trash bags
- A full-length mirror
- Good hangers to replace inefficient ones
- An assortment of organizers—drawers, dividers and rods
- A rolling rack on which to hang clothes

Have Plenty of Uninterrupted Time

Congratulations! You have overcome the first hurdle by deciding to take charge of your mess. If you can afford it and want quicker results, you might consider getting a professional wardrobe consultant. Or you might want to ask a friend to help; if that does not work for you, get ready to roll up your sleeves and get down and dirty.

If you choose to do this task over the weekend, make sure you have at least two 2-3 hour shifts. It is important to have shifts, as this can get tiring. If you choose to work in the morning, have breakfast, wear something comfortable, and stay relaxed. Sometimes the sight of a messy wardrobe can be quite disheartening, but do not get overwhelmed. When you do get tired, take a short break and then keep going, reminding yourself that this is a job you are doing for yourself.

Make Sure You Have Enough Space to De-Clutter

Now, let us start, not with your closet, but with the area around it. I always advise people to have enough space outside and around the closet to help them manage their clutter better. Move all the furniture away from the immediate proximity. Clear the bed. Clean the rug or carpet. Keep trash bags handy. Arrange to have a portable, rolling rack nearby. Keep a full-length mirror around, and lots of organizers. Later in the chapter we will talk about how to divide what's in the closet into various piles to make the de-clutter process easier.

Take Everything Out of the Closet and
Keep Only What You Need (The 20-80 Rule)

Done with space clearing? Good work! Take a few deep breaths. At this stage, you will need help deciding what to keep. You should not be surprised if I tell you that most of us wear 20 percent of our clothes 80 percent of time. So we can safely say that, give or take, almost 80 percent of the space in the closet is taken up by clothes we wear only 15-20 percent of the time.

OK, so you know what those most frequently worn items in your closet look like. What is left is dispensable. It may not be easy, but you have to learn to let go! It is important for your clothes to have breathing space. This will have an impact on your own energy. Dirty, tired clothes can affect the fresh, clean clothes in the closet.

Do not immediately throw out what you do not need. Sell items, or donate them to charity, but only if they are in good shape. Remember, one man's trash is another man's treasure.

To make things easier, divide your clothes into three broad categories: a "Yes" pile, a "No" pile, and a "Maybe" pile. Try on everything you have, see how it fits, looks and feels. Is it a current or a dated garment? Look for snags and holes. Only perfect-looking, well-fitting, current clothes go into the "Yes" pile. The 20 percent you wear frequently do not have to go in the "Yes" pile. Make sure only "good" clothes are in the "Yes" pile, even though they are worn often. Also, classic items definitely belong here.

Into the "No" pile goes everything you have not worn in a year or two. If you have not missed it by now, chances are you will never miss it. Also in this pile put everything torn, worn-out, out-of-fashion, or badly fitting. We are all entitled to have that one pair of slightly oversized jeans, so allow yourself that.

In the "Maybe" pile, keep clothes you are uncertain about or that can be easily altered or repaired. You can show them to an expert or a friend to help you decide.

Now divide the "Yes" pile into categories: Tops and shirts—short sleeves, long sleeves; plain, patterns; formal, casual; sweaters, coats, sweatshirts. Bottoms—pants and skirts, dress clothes, and whatever other categories you want.

Organize the clothes in each category by color. Start with the lightest—white, then gray, then all of the other colors, until you reach black.

Utilize the Space to the Fullest

Use the full height of the closet. Design the closet so everything you need regularly is within reach. Measure the length of your longest piece of clothing; the height of any hanging space should be at least four inches greater than that.

Use the highest and lowest shelves for items you use for special events and unusual weather. Any items kept under 24 inches, you will have to crouch down to reach. Your ski gloves, wide-brim hats, and other items that you rarely wear should ideally be stored on low shelves. Anything you need regularly should be within normal reach.

Anything you normally wear should be kept in easy reach

drawer details

↑ The height of your hanging bar should be 4"
↑ higher than your longest article of clothing

Mix 'n' Match

This rule applies to your clothes, and also to the design of your closet. Shop for closet organizers—consider smaller storage pieces, such as drawers, baskets and chests. There are a number of products you can buy at the stores or online to help you keep your closet organized. Once you have identified space for the items that need hanging, folding, or stacking, divide that space further.

Mix wire racks, wooden shelves, canvas drawers, dividers and baskets, whatever works best in the space you have. It is best to store small items in these. You can organize belts, socks, lingerie, neckties and scarves easily with drawer dividers that are available in different shapes, sizes, and materials like canvas, plastic or wood. Good online stores that carry products to help you organize are www.organize.com, www.getorganized.com, or Bed Bath & Beyond and The Container Store.

Place handbags on a shelf, or in a cubbyhole, facing the same direction and in an upright position. Create divided compartments for handbags, with each compartment containing one color, or a range of colors from light to dark. Closures should be properly buckled, snapped, or tied shut; if the straps or handles can be placed inside the handbag, do so. This will keep the straps from getting entangled with other items in the closet.

TLC

Tender. Loving. Care. Now what's in your wardrobe is what you need. You have cared for what needed attention. After alterations, dry-cleaning and repairs are complete, the next important step is storage. Do not hang everything, and do not fold it all. For example, do not hang knits; always fold them or they'll lose their shape. Always hang linen shirts; they crease easily.

To eliminate odor, you can use bamboo charcoal, usually found in Chinese and Japanese stores. Keeping pieces of cedar in closets is a good idea because of its natural ability to repel insects and discourage mildew. Placing potpourri in the closet will make your clothes smell fresh.

Once you have taken care of your special garments, make sure you do not put things you wear every day, like sweats, sweaters, pajamas, or T-shirts with fresh clothes. Never put these items into drawers, but always hang them up to let them air properly.

Get proper hangers. A wide range of hangers are available today; wooden hangers are recommended for suit jackets, to keep their shape. Use padded ones for your delicate dresses or shirts. Cascading hangers are appropriate if you have lack of space. Shop online or go to a store and ask for help.

If you have a vintage dress or your mother's wedding dress, you will want to preserve and store it in a box, with lots of acid-free tissue paper stuffed around it. Keep it away from direct sunlight and moisture. Or hang it, again using only acid-free tissue paper, and put a muslin cloth cover over it. Never put any plastic on it, as plastic will not let the fiber of the fabric breathe, making the fabric weak and turning it yellow.

Guilty Corner

Ideally, you should get in the habit of immediately folding and hanging everything you take off. But if you find it difficult to do that, have a "guilty corner" and go back to it often. This is a foolproof idea that has helped me and others to whom I've suggested it.

Once you have achieved your dream closet, there is no guarantee it will stay that way. Remember, a neat closet needs a lot of work and attention; if time is scarce, here's what you can do. Allocate some space in (if you are lucky enough to have a walk-in closet) or around (preferably hidden space) the closet where you can put everything after a long day at work. You can use a woven basket or box with a lid, the top of a cabinet, or any space in the closet. But make it a habit to visit this "guilty corner" frequently.

Do not let the pile touch the ceiling or get out of control. You should make it a point to clear it out at least twice a week. By having this "guilty corner," you will keep your closet from getting piled up with clothes, which will take forever to get sorted out.

In Conclusion

If you follow the simple steps suggested in the closet prescription, you will be able to inject new life into your wardrobe. See how easy it is to choose an outfit when your clothing is arranged by style and color? You will never again have to worry about searching for a sweater when it is cold out, or finding the perfect dress for a sunny day.

With the help of these tips, ideas and techniques, the time you will save can be spent doing activities you enjoy. If you feel good, you will look good. Your outside image is all about how you feel on the inside.

DIVYA VASHI
I for Image

(347)330-7713
divya@imagedivya.com
www.imagedivya.com

Divya Vashi trained in image consulting at the Fashion Institute of Technology in New York, enhanced with extensive personal color analysis at the Image Resource Center of New York.

Divya is a member of the Association of Image Consultants International. Because of her passion for personal shopping, her clients enjoy the benefits of her sharp eye to build their seasonal wardrobes. After closet-clearing, a specific list of clothing needs is developed, and with a realistic budget in mind, shopping becomes efficient and fun. Divya believes that you don't have to have a million dollars in the bank to look like a million dollars.

Divya grew up in India. She incorporates the cultural and spiritual values of her country in her work, through techniques such as space clearing, to let positive energies flow in one's surroundings.

She currently divides her time between New Delhi, New York and San Francisco. After working as a reporter and presenter for various media outlets in India (*The Times of India* and *Star News*) and the UK (BBC World Service), Divya decided to use her passion for fashion and her people skills to reinvent herself as an image consultant.

Her clientele consists of CEOs and highly placed executives in the media, actors, models and people at crossroads in their lives.

The Perfect Pack
Dressing Well from a Carry-On
By Julie Kaufman, MBA, AICI FLC

With ever-changing rules for airline baggage, it has become more important than ever to put together a versatile travel wardrobe and know how to pack it in one carry-on piece of luggage. Yes, those overhead bins get crowded, but arriving at your destination at the same time your luggage does is worth it.

In this chapter, you will learn how to choose a travel wardrobe that will be appropriate to wear for every situation and will fit into your carry-on.

Secrets of a Good Travel Wardrobe

If you travel frequently, you probably already have a few pieces of clothing that you know work for you when you're on the road. The garments are probably:

- Dark or neutral color
- Wrinkle-free or wrinkle-resistant fabrics
- Easily folded
- Comfortable
- Fairly basic in style

Do you think you can pack enough clothes for a 10-day trip in your carry-on bag, without living exclusively in black? What if you're going to two different climates? The answer is yes, you can—absolutely. Let me show you how.

Here are the wardrobe goals for a typical business and pleasure trip—the same principles will work for a vacation, excluding any specialized equipment like scuba gear or a ski parka.

In your carry-on bag, we will fit:

- Outfits/suits for business meetings
- Outfits for non-business events
- Outfit(s) for going out in the evening
- Clothes for exercise

All of the aforementioned characteristics of good travel clothes will factor into this wardrobe. However, the first and perhaps most important idea to keep the wardrobe limited, yet flexible, is color. Start with two neutrals and one accent color, chosen from your color palette. If you've never had your colors done, treat yourself and do it right away. You want to do everything you can to know you look great when you are away from home, and learning what colors are most flattering to you is a key strategy in accomplishing that.

As an example, a "winter" might choose black, white and red, or black, white and purple. An "autumn" might choose brown, beige, and orange or green. The objective is to have all of the bottoms work with all of the tops, and to limit the number of purses, accessories, ties for men and pairs of shoes.

I'm going to use the terms "dark neutral," "light neutral," and "dramatic" to describe the colors in this travel wardrobe. For the "winter" mentioned above, the dark neutral would be black, the light neutral would be white, and the dramatic would be red or purple. For the "autumn," the dark neutral would be brown, the light neutral would be beige, and the dramatic would be orange or green.

For our hypothetical mixed business and pleasure trip, we'll need a couple of professional-looking outfits and something for going out to dinner, as well as a casual outfit or two, and exercise clothes.

If you wear suits for business, I suggest you separate them for less dressy events. Pair the suit skirt with a sweater set or different jacket, and pair the suit jacket with non-matching trousers. If you do not need to wear a matching suit for business, use separates for everything. I realize you might have to forgo your favorite dress or jacket. Especially if a specific shoe or handbag is required that won't go with other items you're packing, you'll have to leave it at home.

Here are a few important considerations for always looking great when traveling:

Your objective is to have the flexibility to look appropriately dressed for most any situation, rather than to have all of your favorite outfits with you. To stay within the constraints of carry-on baggage, take your most versatile pieces—four bottoms, up to eight tops, two jackets, various accessories, three pairs of shoes, one exercise outfit, underwear and toiletries.

Every item you take should be capable of doing double duty. Your business-appropriate jacket should also make an outfit over more casual slacks. Your exercise pants can also be appropriate for a Saturday of sightseeing. Your casual sweater should be nice enough to layer under a business outfit for extra warmth.

All of these clothes should be made of fabrics that are wrinkle-resistant, to look good all day, every day. Polyester blends and wool crepe (or light wool suits for men) are good choices. If you're going to several climates, choose clothes that are light enough in weight for the warmer climates, but can be layered for cooler climates.

Make sure you really love the clothes in your travel wardrobe. You're going to wear them a lot. Everything should fit properly and look terrific on you. If you love the clothes, you won't groan as you put on the same pair of pants for the fifth time.

Putting Your Best Travel Wardrobe Together

The first thing to emphasize is that the savvy traveler will take the added step of checking his/her clothes one week before a trip, and send to the cleaners or the laundry anything in need of a touch-up or repair to ensure a fresh, frustration-free start of the trip. Also, there may be clothes you wear only when you travel. If your size has changed since your last business trip or vacation, try everything on just to be sure. You do not want to get to Paris and have your power suit be too small at your big meeting!

The following is a suggested packing list. Use this as a guideline and modify it, based on your itinerary.

Trousers: Three pair. Two pair dark neutral dress pants; one pair jeans or dark neutral casual pants

Skirt: One dark neutral (more, if necessary for your job, but reduce the number of trousers)

Jackets: Two professional-looking jackets that will go with all the bottoms. Ideally, one will be dressier than the other, making one appropriate for going out at night, and the other for wearing both for work and with jeans.

Sweaters/Blouses/Tops: Up to eight. The number depends on the length of the trip. Plan on wearing most of them twice. Each should go with all or most of the bottoms. Each should need laundering or dry cleaning infrequently. At least some should be easy-care, in case you have to wash them in the hotel.

For a cool climate, make sure the tops can be layered. Bring at least one sweater that is thin but warm to layer over another sweater or turtleneck, and under a jacket if necessary. A thin cashmere sweater is perfect for this purpose. Sweater sets can also be very versatile.

Men need fresh shirts daily, whether they wear a suit or sportswear. Therefore, men will need to avail themselves of the hotel laundry frequently to have enough shirts for longer than a four-day trip.

Scarf/Shawl: Choose one good-quality pashmina in a color that goes with everything else. This is a critical piece for bridging various climates. Men might need a wool muffler in cold climates.

Underwear: Up to seven. **Bras:** Up to four. If your trip is longer than seven days, get your wash done halfway through, or hand-wash your panties in the sink every couple of nights. Take a few bras, and wash them in the sink if necessary. A bra with convertible straps will work well under a variety of necklines and sleeve designs.

Sleepwear: One or two. Choose ones that fold small and can be hand-washed and drip-dried. Or, save suitcase space by sleeping in the buff!

Exercise/activity clothes: Shorts or pants and one top, all of which can be washed out easily for repeat use. A wise choice in exercise pants would be a pair that is loose enough and flattering enough to be worn casually on the street. Bathing suit—only if appropriate to the trip. Wear your exercise T-shirt as a cover-up to save space.

Hosiery: One or two pairs of socks for exercise, and three pair of hose. Wash the hose nightly in the sink and drip dry. For men: 5-6 pairs of socks, coordinated to colors of pants.

Shoes: Up to four pairs. One pair of very comfortable shoes, dark neutral, to walk around in all day. Another pair of comfortable shoes, dark neutral, to alternate with the first pair. One pair of dressier shoes, dark neutral, that can be worn with the skirt or the dressiest outfit you're taking. One pair of sneakers, if absolutely necessary for the exercise you'll be doing. If you can exercise in your very comfortable, walking-around shoes, you'll save precious space. If you do choose to take sneakers, wear them on the plane.

Note: All of the shoes should be the color of the dark neutral pants/skirt you're taking. You shouldn't need both black and brown. However, one pair can be "fun" shoes if you have room for them. Here's where men save space. A pair of dress shoes and a pair of casual shoes or sneakers should be sufficient.

Accessories: Take jewelry and scarves (ties for men) to complete outfits. Most accessories take up very little room, compared to extra clothing. You can vary a basic sweater-and-pants outfit with a scarf and belt one day, a great necklace another day, and have two completely different looks.

Handbags: (women) One or two. One daytime bag in your dark neutral color. Optional: One smaller bag that takes up little packing space for evening, dark neutral.

Coat: One if needed. Take one coat that will work in all situations (for example, a warm raincoat with zip-out lining). If you need more warmth, wrap your pashmina around your neck, and wear a wool hat and gloves (they take up much less room than another coat).

Toiletries: All of your liquids and gels must fit into one quart-size plastic bag. Buy travel sizes of deodorant, toothpaste, moisturizers, shaving gel. Get little plastic containers and transfer your other liquids to them. Put all non-liquid/gel items in a cosmetic kit that is soft-sided and no bigger than necessary.

If you lay all of this out on your bed, you're going to think it won't fit. But read on. It will.

Packing

You are allowed one carry-on suitcase and one personal item. Women should use one standard 22-inch rolling bag, and one large, soft-sided tote bag. The tote bag is going to hold a lot, so make sure it has a strap that can hook onto your suitcase or go over your shoulder. Men may prefer a soft-sided, large hanging bag with outside pockets, because they can hang suits in it.

Once you have everything laid out, divide it into three piles. One of the piles will go in your tote, one you will wear, and the rest will go in the suitcase.

Tote Bag Contents

- Laptop and cords
- Paperwork (hopefully not too much—send it ahead with overnight delivery if there's too much to travel with)
- One-quart bag of liquids/gels
- Reading matter
- Pashmina
- Anything else you'll need to use on the plane
- And . . . your daytime handbag

I suggest using a large, inexpensive canvas tote, because it's very sturdy but still flexible enough to fit under the seat. Choose one that is light when empty, to avoid any extra weight when you sling it over your shoulder.

Your Travel Outfit

Unless you must look your best while on the plane—that is, if you are traveling with clients and going straight to a meeting—wear your jeans and sneakers. Even better for perfect packing is to leave the jeans and sneakers at home, and instead travel in your casual clothes and daytime jacket. Avoid large jewelry or a heavy-buckle belt that you'd have to remove at security screening.

Carry-On Suitcase Contents

Everything else must fit in your suitcase. Here are a few tricks to getting it all in:

Take out all removable panels from the suitcase. Each of them makes your packing space smaller and less flexible.

Lay out each pair of trousers on the bed, flat. Put a sweater or top (or two) in the middle of the pant leg. Fold the lower part of the pants over the sweater, then the upper part over the lower part. You now have a pair of pants in thirds around an object that is going to keep the pants from creasing. Put this package neatly into the suitcase, and repeat for the other two pair of pants, the skirt, and the jacket. For the jacket, hold it upright and fold vertically along the back. Lay it down and fold the arms in smoothly. Put a sweater on the lower part. Fold the upper part over the lower, making sure the lapel is smooth.

Stuff socks, underwear, and hosiery into your shoes. You may use a plastic bag or shoe-bag sock around each shoe for cleanliness, but remember, everything extra takes up room. Put the shoes in the corners and down the sides of the bag where there are cavities from the clothes not fitting perfectly. You may need to readjust the pants and jackets to make room for the shoes.

Consider using a plastic bag from the cleaners to separate your good clothes from your shoes. As you travel, you can use the plastic bag as a layer in the suitcase to separate dirty from clean and to keep clothes from wrinkling. Fill in any space with the evening handbag and your jewelry. I strongly recommend against bringing expensive jewelry on any trip.

Wind belts around the perimeter of the suitcase.

Did something not fit? If so, reconsider your selections. Is there anything you can do without? Can you wear another piece or two on the plane or put it in the tote?

Keeping It Clean on the Road

If you're traveling for more than a week, you'll have to wear things more than once. This means having the hotel do some of your laundry, or doing some hand-washing in your hotel sink. If sending your laundry out fits in your budget, by all means do so. Most hotels will take both laundry and dry cleaning in the morning and deliver it back in the evening.

If you want to wash things in the sink, you can bring a smaller-than-three-ounce container of mild soap, or simply use the regular bath soap in the hotel. Remember, this is a functional travel wardrobe, so you're probably not going to be bringing your best silk blouse along. Most washable clothing will survive an occasional encounter with regular soap. Wash the item and rinse it well. Roll it in a towel to remove any excess moisture. Hang it up, preferably with air circulating. Plastic inflatable travel hangers work well, but so does any regular hotel hanger. Avoid wire hangers because they can distort the shoulders of your clothes.

If you know you are going to have to do hand-washing, keep up with it every night or two, assuming you'll be in the hotel long enough for the items to dry. That way you won't have clothes drying all over your hotel room because you've run out of hanging space. You'll also have more options to wear, if almost everything you've brought remains clean.

Clothing that will remain dirty for the remainder of the trip can go in the outside compartment of the suitcase or in a plastic bag, to segregate it from your clean clothes. Dirty items will take up less room if you pack them flat, just as you would have done if they were clean. In fact, for all of your packing, the fewer folds you make in each item, the easier it will be to pack.

There you have it. Now you're ready to attempt The Perfect Pack to ensure you look great anywhere in the world, any time of the day or evening. Perhaps the best part is, you will never lose another checked bag again because all your bags will be with you on the plane. Now you can travel with confidence, knowing you always look your best. Have a wonderful, successful trip!

JULIE KAUFMAN, MBA, AICI FLC
Julie Kaufman Wardrobe Consulting

Clothe yourself with confidence

(650) 323-3970
julie@juliekaufman.com
www.juliekaufman.com

In the belief that appearance is directly related to success, Julie Kaufman is committed to teaching her clients to dress beautifully, helping them look polished, whether at an office, at home or on the road. Julie bases her counsel on both her image training and on her many years of experience in the corporate world.

In addition to individual consultations, Julie's presentations and workshops educate clients on choosing clothing appropriate to their individual bodies and lifestyles. With her tactful yet direct speaking style, she spreads her enthusiasm about dressing well to inspire confidence in the women and men she counsels.

The daughter of a clothing designer, Julie was raised in a fashion-centered household. After spending more than 20 years in advertising and market research, plus earning a master's degree in psychology and an MBA, Julie launched her consulting practice to help people look their best. She finds it rewarding to help others experience the excitement of finding the look that is right for them.

Julie is a certified image consultant through the Association of Image Consultants International, and a color specialist member of Colour Designers International.

Sprinting to the Executive Suite
Your Presence Is Your Competitive Advantage

By Kathryn Lowell, AICI CIP

I work with many business professionals who are stuck. They are educated, know their business, and have great experience in their field. But somehow, on their way up the corporate ladder, these smart, talented individuals stopped getting promoted. They stalled out, or got stuck in a level of management or in a position that did not allow them to demonstrate their full potential. In their frustration, they look for reasons why they can't move ahead. Why, for example, are they passed over while other, seemingly less qualified colleagues move ahead? Although their work product is excellent, they are not promoted to the higher levels in their organization. What happened? Although they are not aware of it, quite simply, they hit the "image ceiling."

You've heard the term "glass ceiling." You've probably even heard about the "grey ceiling"—when Generation X and Generation Y bump up against the large block of Baby Boomers occupying the top levels of corporate America. Well, many of my professional clients hit their own "image ceiling" when they are no longer promotable based on their skill set alone.

Sadly, many of my clients come to me as a last resort, after languishing in unsatisfying lower levels for too long. Why?

They have never learned the qualities of executive presence that are exhibited by top leaders.

How can you move off a career plateau that has lasted longer than you expected? How can you change your career trajectory and rise to the executive positions you desire? No matter what your age or current level in your organization, the following advice will help you understand some of the qualities and characteristics that define those individuals who achieve the highest positions in corporate America.

The Undeniable Foundation

Before we consider the qualities of executive image, let's acknowledge a fundamental requirement of leadership. No amount of "polish" can make up for a lack of integrity. Now, more than ever, you must be a person of character, with strong values and ethics. True executive presence is not about superficial empty suits—no matter how beautiful or expensive. I can make my clients look, sound and act like top business leaders, but if there's not a person of substance and authenticity underneath, in time the image will erode. What is left will not be respected. If you are not a person who honors commitments, tells the truth and respects others, the polished exterior you've cultivated will quickly become transparent. However, if you are a person of character, then adopting the following qualities will allow you to sprint to the executive suite.

The Consistently Refined Appearance

The first strong signal that professionals send about their potential for higher management is their initial appearance. Beth Thorp's chapter on *Executive Style* on page 51, provides a great resource to understand the expectations for an executive wardrobe. However, I find that even those clients who have a good grasp of how to dress may continue to be impeded in four areas:

Failing to upgrade your wardrobe as you move to higher levels. I encourage each of my professional clients to evaluate the quality of their wardrobe. Many people start their careers out of college with debts and a tight budget. Discount stores and department store sales provided their initial business wardrobe. As their income increased, my clients spent more money on fancier cars, homes, electronics and vacations. Unfortunately, however, they often continued their earlier shopping habits of purchasing lower-priced (and lower-quality) clothes. If you are serious about moving to higher levels in business, you must examine your priorities and put additional resources into your appearance. Considering all the time you spend at work, you should be budgeting for better clothes, shoes and accessories. Think elegant styles. Think refined fabrics. Think better craftsmanship. Consider custom-made options, especially shirts for men. These are the details that are expected for executives; upgrading as you move higher shows your understanding of your position.

Settling for mediocre grooming habits. Executive standards of grooming are high. A healthy, vigorous appearance provides a silent message that you are up to the task of running the company. For men and women this means paying attention to your physical condition, and particularly, those parts of your body that need regular maintenance. Standing hair appointments are vital for both men and women. For men, daily shaving is a must, as is using appropriate products to protect, hydrate and condition your skin. For women, resist the temptation to over-process your hair, and especially avoid adding a color or too much highlighting that is clearly not in the realm of natural occurrence. Hair should be cut frequently enough to keep a polished style in place. Women also must learn how to apply makeup that enhances their features, but doesn't draw attention to itself. Think polished, not glam.

Lacking attention to detail. Outdated eyewear. Unpolished shoes. A wrinkled shirt. Pants that drag. An unbuttoned suit jacket. The details always matter for a professional image, and at the executive level, they matter even more. An impeccable visual appearance sends a multitude of positive messages to those around you. It signals that you have a command over the details in your life and that you have high expectations for yourself and your own performance. Purchase a full-length mirror, hang it where you get dressed each day, and scrutinize what you see. Ruthlessly edit your closet, looking for the worn-out, the sloppy, the cheap, and the out-of-style items that are dragging down your visual image. Don't know a tailor? Look one up immediately! Finding someone skilled at clothing alterations is critical to achieving a perfect fit that defines the executive "look." See Colleen Abrie's chapter on *Head to Toe: Details Matter* on page 85 for more on this important topic.

Slipping in and out of professional mode. My mom used to say, "You can't have two sets of manners, one for company and one for the rest of the time." The same goes for your executive image. You can effectively maintain your own visual credibility by defining a standard of appearance and refusing to go below this standard. Avoid the temptation of "jeans day" at work if it means you will slip below your personal standards. Also, unless you have the anonymity of living in a large city or far from work, keep in mind that your executive reputation is always at stake. Even outside the office, it's your duty to preserve your professional brand and consistently demonstrate a powerful appearance.

Exuding Confidence in Every Situation

If we take the concept of executive presence to its highest level, we have "charisma." My challenge in teaching and demonstrating charisma to my clients is that it is difficult to define. We know charisma when we see it (some call charisma the "it factor"). We feel and experience it when we meet those individuals that have this rare quality. Although most of us struggle to define charisma, we often use the word "self-confident" to begin describing this quality of personal attractiveness or interestingness that enables you to influence others. We find people who exhibit self-confidence to be credible and likeable and we find self-confidence is an indispensable quality of leadership. Let's explore a few ways that charismatic people exhibit self-confidence in every situation.

Master confident body language. After forming a quick impression based on your wardrobe and grooming, the next immediate aspect that people notice is your body language. Beverly Samuel's chapter on *The Nine Tenets of Body Language* on page 127 gives you a great start to understanding the power of body language, and I'd like to amplify a couple of key issues. First, watch out for any habits of self-touching, which signal anxiety, insecurity or vulnerability. Touching the face, head, arms and hands as well as putting hands in pockets or hugging oneself (arms folded over the body) negates any message of confidence you are trying to send. Whether speaking to one or one thousand people, find a neutral place for your hands, at your sides or resting on the table in between gestures. When standing, avoid the "fig leaf" position—it's hard to look powerful with your hands crossed over private areas. Next, charismatic people demonstrate "winner posture." Winners have their chests up, their backs straight and their heads up. They keep a balanced stance and avoid leaning, slouching, or crossing their arms or legs. My clients are surprised by how putting themselves in winner posture instantly makes them feel more confident.

Own the room. Confident people stride into a room with the knowledge that they are supposed to be there. Charismatic individuals do one specific thing that sets them apart. They are not looking for a seat, or the buffet, or the bar. Instead, the instant they walk into a room, they are looking to connect with other people. They are the first to initiate a handshake with a friendly smile and a warm word of welcome. They act as connectors, introducing new acquaintances to newcomers, as if each was an old friend. Wherever they are, confident, charismatic individuals seem to take on the role of host, asking questions to draw out a quiet individual, offering to share a table, or providing directions or assistance.

Show energy and get outside yourself. As a true introvert, I'm particularly challenged to keep my energy level high, as I work with people all day and into the evening. Likewise, issues of self-consciousness, ranging from our appearance to doubts of our own intelligence, can impede our ability to appear self-confident as we focus inward on ourselves. If you are like me, as twenty-five to fifty percent of the population may be, it's time to learn how introverted behavior can impact our desire to exhibit true executive presence.

First, understand that our business culture rewards individuals who show extroverted qualities. For introverts, these traits—such as the ability to meet and greet, easily engage in conversations, and give presentations, quickly depletes our energy and we need downtime, away from the stimulation of being around people, to recover.

As introverts, we must learn that our natural tendencies to withdraw or even "zone out" can leave the impression that we lack confidence or are uninterested. As Dr. Marti Olsen Laney writes in her excellent book *The Introvert Advantage* (Workman Publishing Inc., New York, 2002), introverts are likely to "keep energy inside, making it difficult for others to know them" and "avoid crowds and seek quiet" and not "show much facial expression or reaction." If we seek to demonstrate executive presence, we introverts must pay particular attention to how we are perceived, learn how to manage our energy level so we can be "up" at the appropriate times, and find strategies to keep us from withdrawing at the very moments when we should be engaging with others.

Adopting extroverted qualities without feeling overwhelmed can be accomplished over time. I challenge myself and my clients to practice by meeting one new person each day, to schedule our days and weeks for "recovery periods," and to become comfortable attending more events by giving ourselves permission to stay "just long enough" to connect with others. A personal or life coach who understands your personality type can be a good investment to provide the objective feedback and constructive counsel needed to cultivate those important extroverted traits.

Poise that Blends Sophistication with Authenticity

My goal for clients who desire to lead an organization effectively is to help them appear at ease in any given situation. Confident, charismatic individuals have a unique ability to move effortlessly through the layers of social, cultural and economic strata that make up our society. Whether it's joking with the janitorial staff in the hallway one moment and conversing with the board of directors the next, these individuals find ways to gain rapport quickly with everyone they meet. How can we develop our own ability to be at once comfortable and authentic with others? What are the characteristics that allow us to stand out from the crowd and at the same time make us likeable and trustworthy?

Cultivate a natural warmth and openness. The ability to approach each new person and situation with an open mind is a quality that sets others immediately at ease. One reason effective leaders can move comfortably in many circles is because they show a desire to understand and learn from others. They demonstrate a keen adaptability to their circumstances and are never "high-maintenance." They are consistently authentic and likeable because regardless of how high they climb the corporate ladder, they never make others feel inferior or seem to have "all the answers." They don't insulate themselves with "yes" men or women.

We can easily demonstrate our humanity as well as develop personal likeability with one simple act: engage others by asking good questions. Avoid the cliché questions like, "So, what do you do?" or "Where are you from?" or "Where did you go to school?" All these are superficial questions aimed at identifying status. Instead, give people a chance to reveal themselves and their interests more fully, by asking, "What do you enjoy most about your work?" or "What challenges do you face with _____?" or "What advice would you give others about _____?" Sit back and enjoy the thoughtful responses. And remember, one of the easiest ways to delight others is to give compliments. Remember to be specific and sincere, as these are the qualities that make a compliment real and heartfelt.

Demonstrate sophistication beyond your business expertise. People with real presence and charisma are not only interested in others—they are interesting people. People at the top of corporate America are well-traveled, understand cultural differences, appreciate different cuisines, are up on current events, and always demonstrate an intellectual curiosity. For individuals with true executive presence, the world is their comfort zone. For my clients who want to appear more cosmopolitan and well-informed, there has never been an easier time to acquire a wide-ranging education. The Internet brings you the world through videos, blogs, podcasts, and educational sites. Use your commuting time to listen to audio books or tune into satellite radio broadcasts from the BBC or National Public Radio, both of which provide thought-provoking content and model great language usage. Ever want to take a class at Yale or Harvard? Enhance your exercise time by listening to an eminent professor's podcasts for free. Want to understand why NASCAR is the fastest-growing sport in America? Do a little research on the Internet and learn about its appeal. We live in an era where anyone can quickly gain knowledge—use these amazing resources to expand your horizons. Doing so will not only bring you great personal satisfaction, but also make you a fascinating conversationalist, able to find points of connection with everyone you meet.

Demonstrate confidence and clarity in your communication style. Hundreds of books have been written on communication skills for leaders. I find that many basic issues plague my professional clients. The unconscious habit of using filler words (uh, um, like, you know) is an instant credibility killer for any professional. Likewise, a too-simplistic vocabulary restricts your ability to articulate complex ideas. Boosting your word knowledge and broadening your vocabulary by even a few dozen words can improve your verbal image dramatically. Effective leaders also speak clearly—both in tone and volume, and in the meaning of their message. They don't rely on buzzwords, jargon or other off-putting habits like name-dropping to reinforce their worth or position. I encourage my clients to practice speaking in complete sentences, which provides the immediate effect of sounding more intelligent. Finally, remember that executive presence requires that you articulate coherent and persuasive ideas set in a logical sequence. In other words, think before you speak. Good communicators don't rush, and always appear thoughtful in their written and spoken word.

Go Forth and Have Presence

When I graduated from business school, the commencement speaker shocked our class by saying, "Congratulations—now you know 11 percent of what you need to succeed in business." Clearly he meant that no matter how fine our education and how hard we toiled for that graduation day, our ultimate success still depended on actual work experience. I have come to believe that a large part of the missing 89 percent is cultivating a professional presence that makes you confident, likable and engaging. What about you? Are you simply depending on your education or skill set to move ahead? Monitoring and enhancing your image, presence and charisma will be your strategic advantage to move higher in your organization. And most importantly, gaining these qualities will allow you to enjoy self-respect and the genuine admiration of all you meet and lead.

KATHRYN LOWELL, AICI CIP
Image Matters, Inc.

(479) 271-2134
kathryn@imagemattersgroup.com
www.imagemattersgroup.com

When Kathryn Lowell, founder of Image Matters, Inc. graduated from Yale University and started working on Wall Street, she quickly discovered a key to success that was never taught in school—a polished personal image. Throughout her 14-year professional career in finance, emerging market development and entrepreneurship, she studied the attributes of personal image that set apart the highest achievers.

In 2001, Kathryn launched Image Matters, Inc. to advise corporate groups and individuals alike on image enhancement as a stepping stone to higher productivity and personal success. For hundreds of individual clients and for audiences at her popular talks and seminars, she is a trusted expert who demystifies the complexities of wardrobing, grooming, business and social etiquette, interpersonal behavior, and effective public speaking. Kathryn delivers easy-to-understand principles that take people from ordinary to outstanding and from career stagnation to career acceleration.

With an MBA in Finance and Entrepreneurship from UCLA and corporate experience in the U.S. and Europe, Kathryn is uniquely qualified to address the personal image needs of employees at all levels of an organization. Her specialty is assisting career climbers achieve the qualities of executive presence.

The Nine Tenets
of Body Language
How to Increase Your Personal Effectiveness in Every Situation

By Beverly Samuel, MS, AICI FLC

We are communicating all the time, regardless of whether or not we are speaking: when we walk into a meeting, when we acknowledge a colleague with a smile, even when we listen as a client tells us a story. Every time you communicate, you tell something about yourself through your body language. You send out signals for others to read, sometimes congruent with the words you speak and sometimes not. People may have to interpret double messages, which is confusing.

Undoubtedly, you've heard the saying, "You never get a second chance to make a first impression." According to Dr. Albert Mehrabian, UCLA Professor Emeritus of Psychology, a first impression is the whole of three distinctive parts: 55 percent based on appearance and body language, 38 percent on the tone of voice and 7 percent on what is actually said. Whether you find yourself in an interview, at lunch with a client, or in a sales meeting, your overall presentation, including your verbal and nonverbal communication, will significantly affect the impression you make and, very likely, the outcome.

Let's be honest: we're all selling something during a first meeting or a client visit—products, services, or ourselves. There are nine different simple, yet powerful, tenets of nonverbal communication you can enhance to give yourself a competitive advantage: eye contact, smiling, handshakes, showing true interest, voice, gestures, posture, personal space and attire.

Keep in mind that different cultures have different expectations and interpretations of the various aspects of body language. It is important to know those differences when you do business with people from other cultures. This chapter is written for those doing business in North America.

Eye Contact

Your eyes provide communication about your attitude and emotions. They show that you are interested or bored, honest or insincere.

To make good eye contact, don't just gaze into someone's eyes; this will make them uncomfortable. Instead, look anywhere in their eye-nose triangle for two-thirds of the conversation; then look away the other one-third of the time. As an example, during a nine-second conversation, make eye contact for six seconds and look away for three seconds. Practice the flow of conversation and eye contact in the mirror and you will get the hang of it.

When being introduced to several people, make eye contact only with the person whose hand you are shaking, then move on to the next person.

When talking to a group, make eye contact with as many people as possible, so that they feel like you are speaking directly to them. When you consciously make eye contact throughout the room, you appear to be a more credible and confident speaker.

Action: If making eye contact is a challenge for you, play a game. Notice the color of the person's eyes when you make initial eye contact; the exercise will get easier with each person you meet.

Smiling

Your face reflects your inner feelings and moods and can be used to keep someone at bay or put them at ease, creating that positive or negative first impression. When you smile, you give others the impression of a positive, friendly, enthusiastic personality, which is always a great impression to make.

There are many reasons people smile, not always stemming from pleasure. You can tell a genuine smile by looking at the upper half of a person's face. Are their eyes crinkling with pleasure?

Action: If you do not smile much, perhaps because you are often deep in thought or looking at the ground as you walk, make a conscious effort to smile and make eye contact with the people around you.

This behavior will become habitual and will also improve your emotional state. The simple act of smiling actually increases the vitality in your body. Smiling also makes you more approachable.

Handshakes

A handshake can convey important messages about your personality, status, power and intentions: you might appear weak, unassertive, overly submissive, impatient; or strong, self-assured, authoritative and co-operative. Through a handshake, a person may decide that you intend to co-operate with them, submit to them, or dominate them. Thus, the wrong handshake can cause you a lost opportunity—whether a job, a promotion or a business deal.

The co-operative handshake, for example, is firm but not aggressively strong. You will want to fully engage the other person's hand by making sure that the web of your hand is touching theirs, the webs are pointed upward and your palm is flat so as to graze their palm. Pump the person's hand one-to-three times, with your hands equidistant from each of your bodies.

Action: Practice shaking hands, and try to read the other person's type of handshake. Do they seem nervous, relaxed, confident, untrustworthy?

Showing True Interest

*"They may forget what you said, but they will never forget
how you made them feel."*
—**Carl W. Buechner, author**

It is human nature for people to be mostly interested in themselves and to want you to be interested in them, too. Give them what they want and they will hold you in high regard! Show true interest in the other person by using active listening; be attentive and ask questions. Find out what the other person's goals are, and offer ways that you might be able to help them achieve their goals. Don't be busy formulating responses, or you'll miss important details.

Getting good at remembering names makes you memorable and shows others that you have a genuine interest in them. It also makes you more confident in social and business situations.

To remember a name at your initial meeting, repeat it out loud when you first meet someone. Say something like, "Hello, David, it is a pleasure," or "Nice to meet you, Marion." Immediately repeat the name to yourself mentally three times, and then use the name once or twice while conversing with them. Also, make an effort to introduce your new acquaintance to others, thereby forcing yourself to remember their name and again say it out loud. After a meeting or event concludes, run a mental video of everyone you met and their names to solidify the name retention.

Later, you can write down the name, along with important facts or interesting tidbits to help you remember them at your next encounter. When you meet again, re-introduce yourself in case they forgot your name; then they must re-introduce themselves, too. If you forget their name and they have not re-introduced themselves, just say that you cannot remember their name. It will be easier on you than if they discover later that you have no idea what their name is.

The message you convey when remembering someone's name is, "I am interested in you," or "I care about your business."

Action: Practice listening. If you cannot repeat what someone has said, or if you forget what they say immediately after they say it, you are not listening. With practice, you will get better at the skill of listening.

Voice

Look at the sentence, "I did not eat your piece of cake." Say it several times and put emphasis on a different word each time. How many meanings do you come up with? This proves the expression, "It is not what you say, but how you say it." By changing your tone and adding emphasis to different words, you add more expression to your verbal exchanges. It gives others an indication of your attitude about the message, which helps them interpret your meaning. This is especially important when you are talking by phone, or if the other person is visually impaired and unable to read your body language.

During verbal interaction, be sure to match your pace to the other person's. If you talk much slower than they do, they may get bored or impatient. If you are a fast talker, you might tire them out. Either way, they won't be in a hurry to have another conversation with you. Try to match the rate, pitch and rhythm of the other person's voice. You'll want to use this tool especially during phone interviews and sales calls. Be careful about outright mimicry, especially with extremely high or low tones of voice, as you risk offending someone and making a fool of yourself. Stay as much within your normal tone and pitch as possible.

People tend to respond most favorably to mid-range voices. A high voice sends the message of lack of experience or uncertainty. A low voice is fine; however, too low a voice can give the impression that you are angry.

Action. If you think you have a high speaking voice, practice talking in a lower pitch. If you suspect that you talk in a monotone, read nursery rhymes in an exaggerated voice to help animate your voice. If you talk too slowly or quickly, practice speeding up or slowing down.

Gestures

"When trying to persuade people, you have few tools: your words and your actions. Your body either adds strength to your position or weakens it."

—Laura Laaman, "Mastering Body Language Can Help Increase Chances for Success,"
Pittsburgh Business Times— October 15, 2004

Using gestures when talking can add emphasis and feeling to what you are trying to communicate. Overuse can make you appear nervous or out-of-control. Eliminate nervous gestures like covering your mouth, twirling your hair, playing with your fingers or rocking back and forth on the balls of your feet. These gestures are distracting and can be death to your credibility in a meeting, interview or presentation. Practice speaking slowly and clearly while keeping your body still—with pauses for effect. After some practice, you can add gestures to your repertoire of nonverbal communication skills.

Action: The next time you practice a speech, record yourself on videotape and work on your gestures. Add more or use less, as needed. Watching yourself on video is also an excellent tool for noticing how you fare with the other aspects of nonverbal communication.

Posture

"The trick is to come across as poised and alert, yet comfortable and confident," says Granville Toogood, Founder and CEO of Granville Toogood Associates, in his article "The Language of Success for Boom Times or Bust," www.CareerJournal.com—August 29, 2006.

Your posture gives clues about whether you are confident, composed, interested and interesting. It conveys your attitudes, moods and status, establishes trust and helps build rapport, and gives people clues as to how to treat you. Bad posture can distract others from what you are trying to communicate. With good posture, you will be seen as confident and self-assured.

Tall people are regarded as being more successful and powerful than short people. Reflect for a moment on the height of our presidents and CEOs. The point: having good posture can add as much as one inch to your height—for free!

When standing, hold your stomach in, put your shoulders back and down, keep your legs together and your chin up. Do the same when walking, minimizing the space between your legs. Keep your hands at your sides, not in front, as though protecting yourself, or in back, as though you are hiding something.

When sitting, sit upright; keep your back in contact with the rear of your chair and your feet flat on the floor. Women may cross their ankles. Hold your hands flat in your lap. If you are in an interview, keep your knees and body pointed toward the interviewer to show interest.

When sitting, standing, or walking, try to avoid crossing your arms in front of your body. Body language should be interpreted as an overall story, not just by one gesture or posture. However, many people regard crossed arms as a closed attitude, and you don't want to give that impression.

Action: How do you get proper body alignment without looking like a soldier? Practice! Throughout the day, remind yourself to sit up straight or stand up straighter. Good posture is not something that you practice only when someone is looking. Also, the consistent practice of yoga or Pilates® will definitely strengthen your core and ensure excellent posture.

Personal Space

Personal space affects how well a person sends and receives messages, and how well we connect with others. Realize that personal space preferences vary from culture to culture. In western cultures, we tend to value our personal space more than in some other cultures. As an example, an American woman met a European woman to do business. Upon first meeting, after numerous phone conversations, the European woman not only kissed the American's cheeks, but often stood shoulder to shoulder with her. The American's personal space was violated, and she was a bit put off. She eventually got used to it, and you should, too, if you plan to do business internationally. Your goal is to make the other person feel comfortable.

When dealing with westerners, personal space boundaries should be recognized and respected. If you get closer than expected, you can make the other person uneasy; then you'll have trouble getting your message across because he or she will be preoccupied with re-establishing boundaries.

There Are Four Boundaries To Recognize

The intimate zone is 0-to-1.5 feet, which is close enough to touch the other person. If you are not on intimate terms but you need to touch the person, for example, if you are working with them on their appearance or in a medical situation, it might be wise to ask first.

The personal zone is 1.5-to-4 feet. Business conversations take place at about a 3-foot distance. This is close enough to talk, shake hands and read the other person's body language easily.

The social zone is 4-to-10 feet, which is a good distance for talking to small groups of people.

The public zone is 10 feet and beyond. This is the distance used when giving presentations to large groups.

Action: Notice how closely people stand when they are conversing, and consider their relationship. Take note of where you are most comfortable standing or sitting in relation to others when conversing or in a meeting. Not only will you learn about your own comfort level, but, by observing others, you will be able to maintain and encourage comfortable working relationships.

Attire

How you dress is indeed a form of nonverbal communication. Although your attire sends messages about who you are and who you want to be, many people don't give the appropriate attention to what they are wearing or the messages that their clothes are sending.

Action: Refer to the other chapters in this book related to dressing for more information on how to use clothing to improve your self-confidence and your self-esteem.

"In the business arena, it is very important for you to always be aware of what you are communicating nonverbally, not just in an interview or first meeting. Your goal should be to align your verbal and nonverbal communication so that you are always delivering a consistent message. Sending mixed messages leads to roadblocks and misunderstandings, and will ultimately undermine your ability to succeed."

—Sandy Moore, Certified Image Professional and owner of Image Talks, LLC

If your objective is to communicate more effectively and win trust and favor toward the achievement of your goals, then it is vital that you align your words with your actions. You must understand your own nonverbal communication and recognize the communication of others as well. Take the actions outlined here to increase your awareness and effectiveness with nonverbal communication, and pretty soon you may find yourself occupying the corner office.

BEVERLY SAMUEL, MS, AICI FLC
Phoenix Image Institute

Your image speaks long before you do!

(765) 346-3269
beverly@phoeniximageinstitute.com
www.phoeniximageinstitute.com

Beverly believes that sometimes you have to make things happen. As a Certified Image and Etiquette Consultant and Peak Performance Coach, Beverly helps people create the opportunities they want to have through her signature programs on *Body Language and Business Practices, The Art of Business Dining,* and *Reach Your Peak.* She teaches people how to take their vision of themselves from concept to reality by removing the roadblocks to creating and maintaining their image, and she provides techniques that assist her clients in working at their peak all day, every day. Image from the inside out! Her clients receive the tools to market themselves every day—powerfully and consistently.

Beverly, who says, "To be a master, you must train with the masters," trained at the International School of Makeup Artistry; the International Institute for Image Communications; London Image Institute and the Etiquette Institute. She is a member of the Association of Image Consultants International, the American Society for Training and Development, the National Speakers Association and the Etiquette Institute.

Beverly is Editor-in-Chief of the Association of Image Consultants International industry magazine, *Image Update*, which is distributed to 47 countries.

Networking Savvy from the Inside Out
Essential Strategies for Developing Solid Business Relationships

By Brenda Moore-Frazier, MS

Are you one of many professionals who would rather stay at home and read a good book, or watch sci-fi reruns, rather than attend another networking event? Do you occasionally hear about positions, either within your company, or at another firm, that would have been a perfect match for your talent and abilities—after the position has been filled? Many capable and highly qualified professionals cringe at the very idea of attending a gathering where there might not be anyone recognizable in the room or worse yet, where upper-level management might appear.

At times like these, one rarely stops to think that others may be feeling just as uncomfortable. The truth is that not all of us are extroverts, and none of us were born with the automatic ability to make small talk. The good news is that with practice, perseverance, and a change of attitude, we can all learn to network with confidence.

As you speak with people in different professions, networking can mean anything from navigating the Internet to selling vitamins or health drinks. The term networking is used in this chapter to describe a planned process for creating mutually beneficial relationships in order to exchange information, support and resources, and have access to situations and people who can be of assistance professionally. If well-executed, networking can lead to ideal opportunities for those seeking success, both inside and outside their organization. Effective networking might even find you your perfect job, land a huge contract, gain a mentor or make some lifelong friends.

Networking is by no means a short-term process. Sometimes it takes months of investing quality time with associates to establish the trust needed in order to form a true alliance.

Your network can include individuals you have met from all the different aspects of your life—anyone with whom you currently work, members of a professional association or organization to which you belong, people you've met through sharing a common political or religious affiliation, or anyone with whom you happen to be involved through community involvement or volunteer service.

The purpose of this chapter is to provide ideas for developing strategies that will make your networking productive and, hopefully, more enjoyable.

Creating Networking Opportunities

If you are employed, as opposed to having your own business or being between jobs, the first place on your list to research for networking possibilities is within the company where you work. Networking with others within your organization leads to greater visibility in your company, which increases the possibility for career advancement. Many executives agree that when it comes to being promoted, networking efforts may yield better results than working longer hours. Networking is also an invaluable method for keeping up with the inevitable workplace changes. By developing strong allies and knowing exactly what they do within your organization, you will be able to support your company's overall mission or bottom line. As you begin to discover opportunities to fill unmet needs, work collaboratively with employees in other departments, and establish yourself as an expert in your area—you will put yourself in a position to take more responsibility for the management of your future.

Thanks to modern technology, most corporate workers have the potential to interact with hundreds of individuals during the course of a day. Some of these contacts could very likely become network partners for you. Information about specialty networks within your organization and events may be posted on company bulletin boards or even sent to employees via email. Another way of accessing information about company events is by asking fellow workers or inquiring through your company's human resource department.

Organizations and conferences that are specific to your particular industry are also good resources for networking opportunities. Visit the website for the American Society of Association Executives at www.asaecenter.org to search for organizations where you would be a good match. Joining a few of those organizations, and volunteering to serve on committees, provides an excellent way to guarantee an invitation and meet individuals within other organizations who may have access to leaders in your industry.

Events held by specialty professional groups that have members in diverse fields offer an excellent opportunity for networking as well. Alumni associations, and fraternities and sororities are examples of this type of organization. Check your college or university website to get connected.

Volunteering for community-based organizations like the Red Cross or Habitat for Humanity is a wonderful way to become acquainted with members of the community in which you may desire to conduct business.

Become an active member of your local Chamber of Commerce. Chambers are well known for hosting quality events that are well-attended by individuals in a wide variety of businesses.

You can meet others online who can help you attain professional goals. www.linkedin.com and www.spokes.com are popular net-working sites that facilitate connections for the purpose of gathering marketplace information and sharing ideas.

You may consider hosting your own networking event or workshop. Encourage your contacts to invite others from their networks, people who may eventually become allies or networking partners.

Characteristics of the Ideal Networking Partnership

Everyone you meet has something of value to offer. Here, however, is a description of the ideal type of networking partner you want to seek:

Individuals who are positive. Positive people encourage us to persevere when we need the most support. They also speak well of us if our name is mentioned during a conversation.

Individuals who are outgoing. People who enjoy being with and meeting others will naturally have a larger circle of friends and acquaintances than most. Through your association with these individuals you increase the size of your own network.

Individuals who have a good network. Establishing a networking alliance with these individuals can provide you access to relationships with others who can help you meet your objectives.

Individuals who take an interest in you. These individuals will find out what you do and the kind of opportunities you ultimately seek. At networking events, they introduce you to the "right" people, because they have an understanding of exactly what you do and what you need.

Individuals who are trustworthy. You can rest assured that these individuals are looking out for your best interest and will keep you in mind when valuable information comes their way. They have shown that they consistently deliver on their promises and only introduce you to individuals that meet their own high standards.

Be Prepared to Give

Studies have revealed that the most successful networkers are those who make helping others unconditionally their top priority.

There may be times when we feel that we don't have as much to offer, especially if we are starting out in a career or have just recently moved into a new area. However, everyone is looking for ways to help them get ahead. By combining your listening and creativity skills, you may provide a valuable benefit for someone.

Keep your eyes and ears open daily for jobs and positions within your company, or for community organizations seeking new board members. As opportunities arise, you can pass on the information to interested individuals. If you hear by the water cooler that Sheila needs a new housekeeper, put her in touch with Linda, who was raving about her housekeeper to you just last night.

Establish yourself as a resourceful, or go-to person. It is absolutely amazing how others will view you as an expert simply because you know where to send people to have their needs met.

Attempt to learn as much as you can about others. The more knowledgeable you are, the more valuable you will be.

Know What You Need

People have different reasons for networking. It is your responsibility to figure out what you want and be prepared to clearly articulate that at the right time. Your mission may include any of the following goals:

- **Honest feedback** about an idea you have
- **Information** or answers to questions needed in order to complete a project
- **Solutions** for doing something more efficiently
- **Resources** for personal and professional development
- **Contacts** in a particular industry

Preparing for a Networking Event

The first thing you need to know before attending a networking event is the type of function being held and the goals of the event organizers. Is it a fundraiser? Is it a holiday party sponsored by upper management? You do not want to find out after you arrive. If you are not sure, ask.

Set your "agenda" or goals, such as introducing yourself to five new people, or finding a person who can give you specific information about a project you've been working on.

Consider wearing a statement piece that will stand out, such as a one-of-a-kind brooch, or a red handkerchief in your suit pocket—something that will increase your visibility. Your statement piece is also a conversation piece for others.

Rehearse your self-introduction, the response you give when asked, "What do you do?" Make a clear, concise statement and describe the benefit of what you do with enthusiasm and confidence. For example, instead of just saying, "I am a real estate agent," say, "I help people buy their dream homes; I am a real estate agent." With practice, your speech will become a powerful networking tool.

Spend time during the day reading the local newspaper, trade magazine, or company newsletter in order to prepare yourself with current information on issues likely to be discussed during the event. Don't forget to bring more than enough business cards, a small notepad, and a couple of pens in excellent condition.

Mental preparation may be necessary to silence that little voice in the back of your mind saying, "I won't know what to say", or, "What if I don't know anybody there?" Do not allow your "inner critic" to sabotage your plans. Recognize that everyone shows up for the same reason: to seek and offer opportunities. You have something of value to offer, whether information, an idea or an introduction.

Before leaving for your networking event, take one last look in the mirror before you leave. Check for missing buttons, scuff marks on your shoes, lipstick on your teeth, sagging hemlines, or any other detail that could rob you of credibility.

Tips for Navigating the Room

Place your name tag on the right side of your jacket, blouse, or dress bodice so your name will be visible as people shake your hand. If you happen to see some of your friends or co-workers at the event, pay your respects early and then circulate.

Be willing to introduce yourself to others, especially to someone standing by themselves, if there is no one around to do the honors. Also, make sure you introduce yourself to the event host.

Always be pleasant and positive. You will make a better impression on those around you. Be aware of any body language. For more on body language see Beverly Samuel's chapter titled *The Nine Tenets of Body Language* on page 127.

In order to remember something important that was shared, write it on a pad or on the back of the person's business card immediately afterwards. When you send notes to contacts, it is always an impressive gesture to make reference to the conversation you had.

Keeping the Conversation Alive and Pleasant

Find commonality. For example, begin a conversation by asking why the person is attending the function, how they know the host, or how long they have been a member of the hosting organization.

Do not gossip, complain or whine. People naturally gravitate toward those who have positive outlooks.

Be sincerely interested in what a person has to say. People can tell that you are not really listening to them when your eyes roam the room, looking for a more fascinating person to talk with.

Turning the spotlight on the person you are conversing with is an excellent rapport-building strategy. Try to ask questions that require more than a "yes" or "no" response, without appearing to be overly inquisitive or interrogatory.

Business Card Etiquette

Carry your business cards in an attractive business card case. Be sure the information on the card is current. Keep your cards in a convenient place for easy access, but do not give your cards out indiscriminately.

When you are handed a business card, look at it and make an appropriate comment. You may want to write a few identifying notes on the back of the card later. Do not mix cards you collect with your own business cards. Develop a method for organizing the cards for easy retrieval when you get home.

Ending Conversations

The average amount of time you should spend with an individual at a networking event is five minutes, unless you both find yourself in a compelling discussion. If the person seems to have strong potential as a networking partner, follow up with them and ask to meet them at another time. When ending a conversation, always be polite, straightforward and honest. Start by saying, "It has been a pleasure to meet you," and then:

- Refer to your agenda. "I need to speak to ___ before I leave."

- Take the person with you. "Let's get something to drink."

- Introduce him or her to someone else. "Let me introduce you to ___."
- Explain what the next step will be. "I'll call you tomorrow to discuss the project.

Organizing a Follow-Up System

Listed below are types of systems frequently used for easy retrieval of cards or information received at networking events:

- Rolodex
- Notebook with plastic page inserts
- Contact management software, such as Access, or ACT!
- BlackBerry®
- Cell phone

Post-Event Follow-Up and Contact Maintenance

The most important component of networking actually takes place *after* the event: following up with new contacts. There are several ideas that lead to good results.

Sending a handwritten note on quality stationery with an enclosed business card to new contacts within twenty-four hours of the event is an effective gesture to let others know that you are organized and may be interested in developing a long-term networking relationship.

By quickly following up on any promises you may have made, you convey to others that you are reliable.

Devise a realistic schedule for contacting everyone in your network. Create a system that works best for you. For example, decide when or how often you are going to schedule contacts with individuals; then make sure to include with your personal note any news clippings that may be of interest.

Get into the habit of sending holiday and birthday greetings to your contacts. For those of us who need quick and uncomplicated reminders, websites like www.memotome.com and www.birthdayalarm.com are invaluable.

Always send people who provide you with successful business referrals a note, call them on the phone and thank them in person as well. Sending a small gift would also be appropriate.

Final Thoughts

Imagine your network as being your very own personal garden. In order to make it grow, you cultivate the soil, plant the seeds and provide nourishment. Unfortunately, there are going to be a few weeds that need to be pulled so that your success is not sabotaged. As with the flowers in a garden, relationships take time to mature. Through cultivation, patience, and perseverance, your network will strengthen and continue to grow. By respecting every individual you meet, eliminating counterproductive relationships, giving of yourself first without focusing on what you might get back and being proactive, you lay the groundwork for developing mutually beneficial relationships that will help you accomplish your professional goals.

BRENDA MOORE-FRAZIER, MS
Signature Performance
Image & Etiquette LLC

(845) 229-6156
bmfrazier@signatureperformance.net
www.signatureperformance.net

Brenda Moore-Frazier, etiquette columnist for *Hudson Valley Connoisseur* magazine, a Gannett publication, and founder of Signature Performance, has more than 30 years of experience as a speech therapist in upstate New York.

Brenda provides clients with the necessary tools to present themselves to others at their absolute best in both business and social arenas. Specialty areas include communication skills, fine dining, and personal style development. Brenda has presented for organizations such as General Electric, Cendant Mobility, and the Connecticut Association for Healthcare Quality on corporate dress, stress reduction, and networking. Brenda has also used her expertise to create Good Neighbor 101, an etiquette program for community youth that has led to continued collaboration with the Culinary Institute of America in Hyde Park, New York.

A nonjudgmental attitude, expert listening skills, and a keen sense of humor characterize Brenda as a professional with whom clients feel comfortable sharing their vision. Her training approach has been described as creative, energetic, and down-to-earth. Professional affiliations include the Association of Image Consultants International, International Society of Protocol and Etiquette Professionals, and the New York State Speech, Language, and Hearing Association.

Dining for Business Success
What You Don't Know
Can Sabotage Your Image

By Joanne Blake, AICI CIP

I was recently enjoying lunch at an elegant restaurant and glanced around, noticing the other diners in the vicinity of my table. One diner in particular caught my eye. He was a very well-put-together executive businessman whose clothing was obviously expensive and custom-tailored. What drew my attention to him, unfortunately, was the awkward way he held his knife and fork. The man was totally oblivious to the fact that his lack of dining etiquette skill was undermining his otherwise powerful executive image.

Regrettably, an alarming number of businesspeople are blissfully unaware of the table manner mistakes they make that cause them to appear unsophisticated. This will affect others' confidence in them and will in time negatively impact their business and social opportunities.

Even if you think your dining skills are pretty good, I urge you to read this chapter, because the higher you move up in your career, the more essential these skills become. If you don't ensure that your dining skills match your professional image, all the excellent image advice in the rest of this book may be wasted.

I have presented my Dining for Success training program to thousands of business professional groups and individual executives for many years. As a result, I have compiled a list of the most common image mistakes people make while business dining, so that you can avoid them.

Getting Down to Business—Pleasure before Business

Any meal that could affect your business, career or professional success should be considered a business meal. So when should you get down to business?

During many business meals, very little business is actually discussed. The objective is for people to get to know each other better and solidify the business relationship. Other meetings are primarily for doing business. Always make the objective of the meal clear to your guest when issuing your invitation.

Come prepared for small talk and catching up with the other person. Businesspeople usually wait until after the main course is finished before any papers come out and they get down to business. The earliest business should be conducted is after the order is taken so you are not interrupted by the server. Then, just discuss light business topics until the main course is finished. However, the client rules, so whenever they bring up a business topic, take that as a signal that they've had enough small talk.

Ordering Mistakes—Point of Order

If you are dining to make a good impression, I recommend staying away from messy or awkward-to-manage foods. I ask myself, what would a dignitary like a king, queen or president not order? These men and women are called dignitaries because the last thing they want is to lose their dignity by spilling something or looking awkward when they are eating in public.

Therefore, foods you ought to avoid when business dining are:

• Food that may require a special bib, like lobster

• Food that has to be picked up with the fingers, like ribs or corn on the cob

• Food that is designed to slither off your fork, like spaghetti; better to choose sturdier pastas, like penne or tortellini.

Course Pairing

You know how awkward it feels if you are eating and no one else at the table is. To avoid this, order the same progression of food so you can accompany your dinner partner, course by course. A savvy host always orders last, for the tactical reason of ensuring that you are eating the same courses as your guest. That means if the guest orders a salad, you order either a soup or a salad to accompany them. Even if you don't feel like having an appetizer, order one if your guest does. Nothing says you have to finish it. The same rule applies for beverages. If your guest orders something to drink, always accompany them with a beverage of your choice, not necessarily alcohol.

The Tortoise and the Hare

There is not much sense in ordering the same progression of food that your dining partners do if you are going to gulp yours down and then sit and watch them eat slowly. If you do tend to eat faster than others, consciously slow down your pace.

Some people are just slow diners, and it can be excruciating to watch one person dawdle over their course when everyone else is done. If you notice that you've lagged behind your dinner companions, you can simply place your silverware in the finished position and let the server know that you're done. Your mother isn't there to insist you finish everything on your plate!

Saving Face—and Your Clothing

Oftentimes, people do not seem to know what they should be doing with their napkin. The napkin has two main uses: to protect your clothing should any food spill, and to wipe your mouth before you talk or take a drink.

Get into the habit of putting the napkin on your lap shortly after you sit down at the table. If you don't, sure enough, Murphy's Law and the law of gravity seem to conspire to make you spill something on your lap.

If you have to leave the table during the meal, place your napkin on the chair seat and push your chair in, out of the way. The napkin is never placed back on the table until the end of the meal, when everyone is finished. The reason for this practice is to avoid having a stained or messy napkin in everyone's view while they're eating. At the end of the meal, the napkin is loosely folded and placed at the left of your dinner setting.

Before you speak to someone, touch your napkin to your lips. This not only prevents you from speaking with food particles stuck to your lips, but also gives you extra time to finish chewing before speaking. Before you take a drink, dab your lips so you don't leave food on the glass. This is another habit that needs to be practiced at home so you won't forget it when dining in public.

Silverware Savvy

If you only read one part of this chapter, this is the section to read. I can't overemphasize that how you handle your silverware immediately signals to others whether you have good or poor table manners.

It is becoming exceedingly common to see businesspeople, like the well-dressed executive in our opening paragraph, holding their knives and forks like little children who are just learning to dine. Unfortunately, that awkward behavior is right out there for everyone to see.

Blue Chip Holdings

If you want your table manners to look as good as the rest of your professional image, you need to test how you look when holding your knife and fork.

Right now, go to the kitchen and get a knife and fork. Hold them the same way you normally would and pretend to cut something on your plate.

Now compare them to the following illustrations:

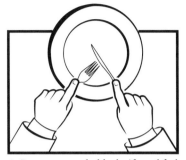 

A. Proper way to hold a knife and fork   **B.** Proper way from below

They should look like diagram A. Your index or pointing fingers should extend down the handles. Your forearms and wrists should not be cocked at an angle but should be fairly straight. Your right and left hand should look similar.

Turn your hands over to see if the handles nestle easily in the palms of your hands as in diagram B. Each hand should almost be a mirror image of the other.

If you hold the knife and fork in any other manner, you will look awkward to other people when you dine. Practice until it becomes second nature to hold a knife and fork this way while cutting your food.

American Style or Continental Style—
Which Option is Right for You?

In North America, it is accepted that there are two "proper" styles of eating. Yet 80 percent of the businesspeople in my dining seminars have no idea which style they use. When you don't know which style you use, how can you be sure that you're doing it correctly?

If the knife stays in your right hand and the fork stays in your left hand as you cut and eat the food, you use the Continental style. If you put your knife down after cutting and move the fork to your right hand for eating, you use the American style.

Pay attention to other diners to see which style appeals most to you. Left-handed diners tell me that the Continental style is easier for them to use.

Whatever style you choose, make sure that you practice it at home so you don't appear awkward when dining in public. Using a method other than the American or Continental style will make you stand out in a negative way when dining with others.

Style Mistakes—Out of Style

Let's examine some of the image faux pas that are common to each style. The American style can be noisy if you clang your knife against the plate when changing hands. You don't want to be changing hands constantly throughout the meal, so cut up no more than three pieces of meat before switching hands. Remember to cut small pieces so that you're not stuffing your mouth.

Another problem with the American style is that people get lazy using it. They don't want to keep switching back and forth, so they start to use the fork to cut things with its edge, or worse, they use their fingers to push food onto their fork.

Because the utensils do not change from hand to hand, the Continental style is more efficient. You need to be careful so that you don't get too far ahead and outpace your American-style dining companions, though. Since the knife and fork stay in your hands while eating, people easily make the mistake of gesturing with their silverware and waving their knife and fork around while talking.

Proper Signals—Signal Sophistication

Have you ever had a server take your plate away before you were done, or ask you if you were finished when you were not? This may have occurred because you inadvertently gave the wrong signal with your knife and fork.

The resting position is used to signal that you are pausing during the meal and that you do not want to have your plate removed just yet. Your knife rests on the right edge of the plate at approximately the 4 or 5 o'clock position, with the blade facing inward. Your fork rests in roughly the same position on the left side of the plate.

The finished position signals that you are done with the course and that your plate can be removed. The fork and knife are placed side by side on the right side of your plate at approximately the 5 o'clock position. The fork is on the inside and the knife on the outside with the blade facing inward. These positions may vary slightly, depending on how much food remains on your plate.

Dining Confidential—What Your Best Friend Won't Tell You

I was about to deliver a dining presentation to a group of midlevel executives of a national firm and their spouses. Moments before I was set to begin, the CFO's wife approached me tentatively and said, "I want to make sure you address something that my husband is guilty of." "What's that?" I asked. "Talking with his mouth full," she replied. I assured her I would be sure to speak about this issue, as it's one that people will notice about their dining companions.

Let's deal with a few of these image-spoiling faux pas that are becoming more common in executive dining rooms. These are things your best friends and colleagues may note, but won't tell you because they don't want to jeopardize their working or personal relationship with you.

Straight Up Isn't Just for Martinis

Many people appear awkward while dining because they hunch over their meals. You look much better physically when you sit up straight at the table. This posture also prevents you from making other dining image slipups.

People who use the American style of eating are much more likely to hunch over their food, especially if they make the mistake of placing their left forearm or elbow on the table while eating with the fork in their right hand. This awkwardness is the main reason for the rule about "elbows should be off the table while eating."

Keeping your chair pulled in prevents food from falling onto your lap, and makes it easier to sit up straight. Your back should be against the back of the chair, and your elbows kept tucked in against your sides. Practicing, and being aware of your erect posture, also stops you from making the mistake of lowering your mouth to the food, rather than raising the food to your mouth.

Compulsive Behaviors—Moi?

I was once hosting an executive at a restaurant that specialized in exotic meats like wild game. Both of us had ordered the venison, but I noticed my guest had eaten most of everything on his plate except the meat. I was concerned and asked him if the venison was to his liking. He told me it was, but that he always preferred to eat his meat last.

Behaviors that may seem compulsive to others should be avoided. This includes eating all of one item on your plate before moving to the next, and the often-seen practice of cutting up all your food at one time before you start to eat. These behaviors remind others of the dining peculiarities of children, which is surely not the impression most of us aim for when business dining.

Grooming for Failure

Women who apply makeup and men who comb their hair or pick their teeth at the table may think they're improving their looks, but they're certainly not improving their image. Anything that falls under the heading of grooming should be done in the privacy of the restroom, far away from the table.

BlackBerry Crumble—Electronic Disconnect

You may think it shows what a busy, connected person you are if you take calls or text while dining with others, but this activity can actually cause your professional image to crumble. Part of having a classy, gracious image is focusing on your dining companions to show them respect. Remember that dining, even for business, is about socializing and building or solidifying a relationship with the person you're dining with.

Your Personality is the Featured Dish

A first meal with someone is like creating a first impression, even if you've interacted with them in other business situations. If you don't have much history with the people you're dining with, they will be looking for clues to your character and a taste of how you operate by the way you behave with the restaurant staff.

Relationships develop better when everyone has a nice time and enjoys their meal. If you are the host, it is up to you to make certain that everyone is at ease and that their needs are met by inquiring how they are enjoying their food. You should be the one to request missing forks, additional rolls, or more coffee. It's your responsibility to oversee your guests' enjoyment in a proactive and firm, yet always polite, manner.

Don't be rude to the wait-staff—for example, snapping your fingers to gain their attention. Try to avoid making a scene. Any sort of confrontation at the table will put a damper on the whole meal. If the service is not up to standard or there is a particular issue, excuse yourself and deal with the staff privately.

This also has a bearing on how you should deal with your own faux pas. How you handle mistakes reveals more about your true leadership and personality traits than when things run smoothly. Such a situation should demonstrate your "coolness under fire" or "grace under pressure." If you spill something like a glass of wine, for example, don't make a big fuss. Use your napkin to blot up the spill and then get the server's attention to assist in the clean-up and to bring you a new napkin and drink.

For this or any other inadvertent mistake, simply apologize once and then let it go. Using self-deprecating humor like "I'm having one of those days" can help alleviate any embarrassment, demonstrate that it's not a big issue, and that you don't take yourself too seriously.

Dine in as if You're Dining Out

Your dining skills can, and should, augment your overall professional image. Looking good while dining is a goal that requires commitment. Invest in the time and training to practice your skills at home daily so you don't slide back into bad habits while dining with others. That way, you will increase your confidence, power and influence as people subconsciously recognize that your sophistication and polished executive image are in evidence at the dining table with every meal.

JOANNE BLAKE, AICI CIP
Style for Success
Speaker and Trainer
Business Image, Etiquette and Dining

(780) 472-0767
joanneblake@styleforsuccess.com
www.styleforsuccess.com

Joanne Blake is a professional speaker and internationally Certified Image Professional. As a member of the Canadian Association of Professional Speakers, Joanne's warm, humorous approach enlivens conferences and in-house training. She has been setting the standard in business etiquette, networking, and professional image training in Canada for almost 20 years.

Her company, Style for Success, works with business professionals and organizations across the country, providing valuable tools for working and living more successfully. A valued commentator for television and radio, Joanne has been featured in national and international publications such as *The Globe & Mail* and *The New York Times.*

As a way to discreetly assist those wanting to improve their dining skills and achieve greater confidence at the table, Joanne was inspired to create Dining for Success, an on-line video training program. MBA and business schools and companies worldwide are using this resource to enhance careers and business success.

Navigating the Corporate Cocktail Party

With Style and Grace

By Amy Elizabeth Casson, AICI FLC

Some professionals are born to schmooze. They love networking. They enter a room with confidence, smile broadly as they approach people, shake hands with ease and navigate their way around the room like they own it.

But some of the same people who thrive at business networking events cringe at the thought of having to attend their company's social functions. They enter the room slouched over and avoiding eye contact, appearing to be holding up the wall or spending an incredible amount of time at the buffet table.

It is time for those of you who dread the social business function to set aside your fear and worry no more. The following three steps will help you master the business cocktail party with style and grace, allowing you to seize the endless opportunities that it offers.

Pre-Party: Develop a Positive Mindset

Social business functions can do wonders for your career. It is a time when people are more relaxed and open to meeting others. In today's fast-paced business world, social functions offer the business executive an opportunity to network and socialize—an opportunity that does not happen throughout the rest of the business day.

You must develop a positive mindset before attending a cocktail party. Think about how many wonderful and interesting people you are going to meet. Develop a mental checklist of key people with whom you want to connect, and stick with it. Believe that other attendees will want to meet you, that you have something to offer them. And smile every time you think about the party. Simply smiling will lead to a positive mindset.

Prepare a Self-Introduction

Prepare a one-to-two sentence self-introduction. Rehearse so it flows easily, but don't over-rehearse or it might sound canned.

The best introductions for social business functions are those that include your name and something about you that connects you to the others in the room. The whole idea behind an introduction is to start the conversation rolling. If the person with whom you are speaking is intrigued by your introduction or in some way feels connected to you, they will be apt to continue the conversation.

For example, two professionals, a lawyer and a financial advisor, are attending a cocktail party for a local charity. The lawyer might introduce himself by saying, "Hi, my name is Christopher. I'm a corporate lawyer for the law firm Smith, Smith and Smith. Doesn't this charity do great work for the community?" The financial advisor, Jeff, might respond by saying, "Absolutely. My name is Jeff and I'm a financial advisor for Highroad Asset Management. I sit on the board of this charity and I am always amazed at how many people it helps on a daily basis."

The conversation will flow from there because they have made a connection by talking about the charity.

Practice Your Handshake

Handshakes say a lot about a person. Bone-crushing handshakes leave the impression that you are power-hungry, insensitive and uncaring about others. Limp handshakes suggest you are weak and subservient. The best handshakes are those that are firm but not overpowering. Never grab the person's hand, elbow or shoulder with your other hand unless you know them well. And gentlemen, always treat a woman with respect when shaking hands. Shake a woman's hand the same way you would shake a man's hand—web to web for two to three seconds making eye contact the entire time.

Test-Run Your Outfit

If you were a product, your clothes would be your packaging. What would your clothes say about you? Would they effectively tell your story? If someone were to meet you for the first time at a cocktail party, would they be able to accurately define your personal attributes within twenty seconds-to-two minutes?

Choosing what to wear to a cocktail party takes time and effort. Ask the host for dress code clarification if the invitation does not identify the dress code. Or, use the starting time of the event as a dress code guideline if you are unable to connect with the host. Ideal cocktail party attire changes with the start time of the event.

A 5 p.m. start indicates that the host is expecting attendees to wear their office attire to the event. There is no time to go home to change, but this doesn't mean you wear khakis to a cocktail party. Plan to wear a suit that day to the office. Dark-colored suits (black, navy and gray) are considered more formal than light-colored suits. Choose a shirt—dress shirt for men, blouse for women—that will hold up and not appear wrinkled by the end of the day. Ladies, avoid wearing linen.

Wear comfortable shoes, because you will be standing throughout the evening. Ladies, wear a basic pump, sling-back or kitten heel. Gentlemen, choose a lace-up. And make sure your shoes are polished.

You might want to add some accessories to make your business suit appear more evening-like. Gentlemen, you may want to change your leather-band watch to a metal watch. Ladies, you may want to add a fabulous beaded necklace to add some elegance to your suit. Bring your accessories to the office in the morning and put them on before you leave for the party.

A 6 p.m. start indicates you may or may not have time to go home to change. If you don't have time to change at home, bring evening-type clothes with you to the office in the morning. Ladies, ditch the cotton blouse for a satin blouse. Add some shimmering accessories to bring life to your business suit. Throw a silky wrap over your shoulder instead of your traditional overcoat. And put your hair up in an up-do if possible. Gentlemen, wear an Egyptian cotton shirt with a colorful, evening-like tie. Add cufflinks to step up the elegance of your outfit.

A 7 p.m. start suggests you go home and change for the event. Wear traditional cocktail party attire—cocktail party dress for ladies and a dark suit and tie for men.

Once you have decided what to wear, try on your outfit to ensure a proper fit. Look in the mirror and ask yourself if your outfit effectively represents you. Take care of the details. Make sure there are no stains, tears or scuffs. Set aside the right accessories to make your outfit shine. Details are important when it comes to making positive impressions at business functions.

Just as products are tested before they leave the manufacturer, you want to "test" your outfit before wearing it to a social business function. Try your outfit on a few days ahead of time and wear it for the same amount of time you plan to be at the function. This will give you confidence that your outfit will work well at the big event. This also gives you time to remedy any outfit challenges.

Read, Read and Read Some More

Find out who is attending the cocktail party and then read up on them. Start your search by "Googling" the names of attendees—you will be amazed at the information you can find about a person by simply entering their name in an online search.

If you are attending a company party, know the key players and decision makers. Be knowledgeable about the direction of the department or company so you can intelligently contribute to con-versations and show you care.

Read journals, association newsletters and search blogs if you are attending an association cocktail party. The more you know about the industry, the better you will be able to connect to others at the party.

The Party—Enter the Room Like You Own It

Entering a room with confidence should not be a problem for those who have adapted a positive mindset. Confidence is conveyed through body language and voice quality. Check your posture before entering the room. Are you holding your shoulders back? Are you standing straight? Is your head horizontal to the floor and not tilted? Are your arms lying comfortably by your sides? Adjusting your body language will help you appear confident, relaxed and open to conversation. Read Beverly Samuel's chapter on *The Nine Tenets of Body Language* on page 127 for more on this important subject.

Now check your facial expression. Are you smiling? Do your eyes look like they are laughing? Do you appear as though you are happy to be at this function? Smiling releases endorphins in your body and helps other people feel at ease and welcomed.

What do you do once you have entered the room? Do you quickly run to the buffet table or bar? Do you stand by the doorway in hopes that someone will approach you? Or do you start the mingling process, immediately looking for opportunities to connect with individuals? The sooner you jump in, the easier it will be in the long run.

Mingling is an art. The best people to approach when you first enter a room are those who are on their own, and therefore will be thankful for your company, or those in groups of three or more. Approaching people who are in groups of two can be awkward, as these people may be conversing confidentially and do not want to be interrupted.

Wait for the conversation to subside, if you are approaching a group of three or more, and then boldly introduce yourself to the group. Remember your rehearsed self-introduction. Make eye contact with someone in the group and offer a warm, sincere smile. Extend your hand when you make eye contact with a group member. The group should welcome you by physically making space for you and by including you in their conversation. Move on to another group if they do not include you. And tell yourself that they do not know what they are missing by not including you.

Converse with Class

Silence can be golden, but not necessarily at a cocktail party. Do not panic if the conversation lulls for a few seconds. Instead, think back to the information you culled prior to the event through your hours of research.

Conversing with class means choosing topics that most individuals will be able to contribute to, that make people feel good about themselves. It means injecting positive energy into your circle, rather than sucking the life out of it.

Choose your topics wisely. Avoid highly emotional topics that can offend some individuals, but also avoid topics that will put people to sleep. Politics and religion can be offensive to some, if you have differing opinions. Conversing about the weather can be incredibly boring, unless you are experiencing unusual weather. Highly emotional or boring topics will end a conversation quickly.

Common experience is always a good conversation starter. For example, talking about the venue, the view, the food (but avoid complaining about it), and the company or organization that is hosting the event are topics on which everyone in the circle can comment.

A conversation should be like a tennis match. You make a comment, then the other person responds, you make another comment, and so on. The conversation should flow back and forth, with neither party monopolizing it.

Typical conversations at cocktail parties should last between 10 and 15 minutes. It is important to continue to circulate and meet other people at the event. After all, you are there to build your network and meet other fascinating people.

Always pay attention to the person with whom you are speaking. The best way to make a great first impression is to sincerely look as though you are interested in what he or she has to say. If you look like you are "working" the room—always looking over the person's shoulder for someone more interesting—you are behaving improperly and you will not win many friends.

Leaving a conversation gracefully is easier than you may think. Wait until you have made a comment, then simply smile and extend your hand. Tell them it's been a pleasure speaking with them and move on. Or, you may want to bring your new acquaintance along and introduce them to your friends. Your new acquaintance will be forever grateful to you for taking them along—especially if they arrived alone.

Juggle Food and Drinks with Ease

We have all experienced the embarrassment of someone offering their hand and not being able to shake hands because we are juggling food and drink. The best way to avoid this situation is to keep your drink in your left hand and your food in your right hand. When someone offers to shake your hand, transfer your food to your left hand. Or if there is a table close by, place your food on the table momentarily and shake their hand.

Always keep the amount of food in your hand to a minimum. This will make the transfer of food to your drink hand much easier.

Make sure your hands are clean. Wipe your hands on a napkin or, if there are no napkins available, casually rub your hand against your clothes before you shake hands.

Refrain from speaking if you have food in your mouth. Wait until you have swallowed, then speak.

To Flirt or Not to Flirt

Flirting does not belong at a corporate event. Period. You are still on business time, even if the hour does not suggest so. This does not mean that you have to refrain from connecting with people—simply leave the amorous behavior (kissing, hugging, holding hands) for after the party when you two are alone. If you are having an office romance, it is best to keep this relationship a secret from your co-workers until you become serious. That way if the romance sours, co-workers will not feel awkward being around the two of you.

Cocktail parties are no excuse for rude, flirtatious, gluttonous or intoxicated behavior. You are doing yourself a disservice, and could perhaps harm your business reputation if things get out of hand. All of us have witnessed someone misbehaving at some point in our careers. It is almost impossible to regain your professional image once you have made a negative impression with your peers and colleagues.

Arriving and Departing

Arrive at the cocktail party shortly after the indicated start hour. Showing up on time gives the impression that you are prompt and organized—two characteristics that are important in business. You do not want to arrive twenty minutes before it is time to leave. Arriving late makes the host feel obligated to stay longer and socialize with you.

Stay at the party for at least an hour. The host thanks everyone for coming and acknowledges certain guests and team members at the hour mark. So it's important that you are there to hear what the host says—especially if you are one of the people who are being acknowledged. Thank your host before leaving; say that you had a great time and enjoyed getting to know your colleagues.

If you are hosting the event—whether in the office, at your home or at a different venue—it is your responsibility to make your guests feel welcome. Make your way around the room and shake hands with all of your guests. Try not to preoccupy yourself with particular attendees.

Post Party—Stay Connected

Send a handwritten thank-you note to your host within a couple of days of attending the cocktail party. Sending a handwritten note is far more gracious than a thank-you by email. Handwritten notes take time and effort. You have to buy the stationery, write the note, buy a stamp, and physically mail the envelope. These steps take effort and suggest to your host that he or she is important to you. Making others feel important is the number one rule of etiquette.

Send emails to those whom you met at the party. Tell them it was wonderful to meet them and that you would be thrilled to keep in touch. Make a lunch appointment with anyone you want to get to know better.

Staying connected takes time and effort, but it can pay dividends in the long run.

We live in a fast-paced society where first impressions are formulated within 20 seconds or less. Knowing how to navigate a cocktail party with ease helps others develop a positive impression of you. In today's business world, the more people you impress with your civilized behavior, the higher your chance of success.

AMY ELIZABETH CASSON, AICI FLC
Polished Image

Helping professionals win in business

519-872-8249
amyelizabethcasson@polishedimage.ca
www.polishedimage.ca

Leading certified corporate image, etiquette and communications consultant Amy Elizabeth Casson believes that a polished image greatly influences whether or not a professional will succeed in business. As a result, she specializes in polishing the presence of professionals across North America so they can differentiate themselves and their companies from the competition, effectively build rapport with potential and existing clients, and exude confidence and charisma.

Since 2004, Ms. Casson has polished the presence of thousands of corporate clients, including Deloitte Consulting, Investors' Group, Nestle Canada, Johnson & Johnson and TLC Stores, through workshops, seminars, e-learning solutions and one-on-one training. Her flagship programs—"Professional Presence University" and "Branding Me"—have garnered rave reviews from both the corporate and educational worlds.

Ms. Casson is the career image consultant for www.monster.ca, Canada's leading job search portal. She has been quoted in newspapers, including the *National Post*, and has appeared on television programs and radio shows. She is a certified image consultant, personal brand strategist, DiSC personality analyst and member of the Association of Image Consultants International. As an added benefit to her corporate clients, Ms. Casson has previously worked as a marketing manager for a Fortune 500 company.

Tech Etiquette
Perfecting the Art of Modern Communication
By Peggy M. Parks, AICI CIP

Welcome to the new frontier of modern communication. According to a 2007 Pew study, 73 percent of U.S. adults own a cell phone, 68 percent own a desktop computer, 30 percent have a laptop, 73 percent connect to the Internet, 37 percent regularly use instant messaging and 41 percent send text messages from their cell phones. Traditional modes of communication have been replaced by this new digital medium, and being able to keep up is crucial to maintaining a forward-thinking, competent, and plugged-in executive image.

Consider, for example, the 2008 presidential election. Barack Obama and his advisers were able to reach voters and usher in a message of change through text messages, emails and sleek web campaigns. By contrast, John McCain's admission that he didn't use email and rarely used the Internet was criticized as seeming out of touch in this wired age.

But it's just not enough to be able to understand and use these high-tech gadgets and applications. It's important to use them intelligently. How you, your character, your credibility and your levels of professionalism and ethics are perceived will be judged by how you choose to communicate with others via these current means. The time has come in this technological revolution for basic guidelines to be laid down and followed. The time has come for "tech etiquette."

What is tech etiquette? It's the determination to practice awareness and considerate behavior whether you're jotting off a quick email or sending a text on your new iPhone. It's a reminder that courtesy and professionalism don't stop at the information superhighway. Also, tech etiquette is a way to build a successful, capable image in this competitive world.

This chapter will guide you through the fundamental "rules of engagement" for navigating through a wired world via email and text messaging. Implementing them into your daily routine will not only pave the way for smooth communication, but also help you gain valuable respect.

Email

Long gone are the days when a manager would dictate a letter to his secretary, who would then transcribe her shorthand to a beautifully typed letter. Instead, email is the standard means of communication in business today. That's why email etiquette is so important. Each email we send is a little branding message that represents who we are and how we carry ourselves—make it count.

Branding Yourself Via Email

Think of an email as you might a business card. Does it look tasteful and professional? Does it provide pertinent contact information? Is it worthy of your position—or the position you hope to attain?

For starters, consider your email account address. Most companies will assign you a standard address, but if you are job-hunting or work freelance, avoid the urge to use a cutesy email address that you think showcases your personality.

"Bikerchick67" or "Dixiebelle" may sound fun, but they aren't appropriate for business communications. Instead, go the extra mile by purchasing a domain with your name or brand. For example, janesmith@janesmith.com or janesmith@smithconsulting.com sound infinitely more professional and credible than janesmith@gmail.com.

Next, add an email signature to your email template. Since you cannot give the person to whom you are writing a business card with your contact information, you need to have all this in your email signature. Include your full name, professional title, company name, telephone number, fax, and business address.

Finally, steer clear of jazzing up your email with colorful text, dark backgrounds, and cutesy graphics—they undermine your professional image and can be very distracting. Every once in a while I receive emails that have so much "stuff" in them, it is difficult to concentrate on the words. That said, a small, tasteful company logo as part of your signature is perfectly fine, and is a great way to brand yourself.

Effective Email Language

Many people may have trouble expressing themselves through writing, but following some simple guidelines will help you communicate clearly and intelligently.

First, be sure to use a salutation in your email. Proper grammar and spelling are also important, as typos show a lack of care and respect. Always spell check your email, proofread for errors, capitalize your sentences and use appropriate punctuation and grammar. It is time well spent. Misspelled words and bad grammar are very distracting—it's the equivalent of having spinach in your teeth. People won't listen to what you say; they'll be distracted by the spinach.

Try to treat your emails as you might a company memo. They should be professional but not stiff, and to the point. If you're not the writer type, just include a quick summary line and list bullet points so it is clear what you are trying to say.

That said, do not make a habit of answering all your emails with a canned reply. I've seen people send out a reply to all emails: "Thank you for your email. I'll get back to you as soon as I can." You lose credibility by doing this and make people feel they are not important enough to you.

Make sure you don't use incomprehensible language such as abbreviations and acronyms. Avoid TTYLs, LOLs, and childish smiley faces, no matter what.

Always end your emails with "thank you," "sincerely," "best regards," and so on. Each email you send as an electronic letter, and this is the way you need to treat it. Would you meet with someone in person and not say goodbye at the end of the meeting? No. Always show that you are courteous and a pleasure to communicate with.

Avoiding Embarrassing No-No's and Annoyances

We've all heard corporate horror stories of someone drafting a quick rant to a colleague about a boss or troublesome client, only to realize when it's too late that the email went out to the wrong person. This isn't just careless—it could get you fired. You can never be too careful or conscientious when dealing with emails. Think before you send.

For instance, if you are writing an email to multiple people, it's important to know the difference between cc'ing, in which it is clear who is being copied, and bcc'ing, in which another recipient receives the email but stays hidden. If you are sending a mass email to a large list of diverse contacts, use the bcc function. The recipients will appreciate the privacy, and it will protect you from sharing your hard-earned contacts with the world.

When responding to a mass email, avoid using the "reply all" button unless every single person on the list needs your response. Otherwise, just reply to the original sender. Many people get irritated reading emails that have no relevance to them.

The same can be said of forwarding emails. Do not forward emails without the writer's consent, and do not copy a message or attachments belonging to another user without permission of the originator. If you do not ask permission first, you may be infringing on copyright laws. And please steer clear of sending "humorous" or chain letter-type forwards on company time. They're tiresome, distracting, unprofessional and clog up people's in-boxes.

When sending an email, do not attach unnecessary files. This can be annoying to the recipient and even bring down their email system. Only send attachments when they are necessary and productive, or are specifically requested.

All emails should be replied to within at least 24 hours and preferably within the same working day. If you don't have all the answers, send an email back stating that you have received the email and that you will get back to the sender. This will put your client's mind at rest and they will be more patient. If you ignore an email, you are telling your client that he or she is not important to you.

When you know you will be away from the office, or are working on a deadline, make sure you use auto reply messages. You do not want a client to be expecting a timely reply from you if you're on vacation for two weeks. He or she will feel ignored and will go to your competitor. Set an auto reply message just before you leave the office and make sure you turn it off as soon as you return, as it's annoying and shows lack of oversight to receive a message from you on January 15 stating that you will be out until January 12. The same thing goes for outgoing voicemail messages.

Your auto response should be brief. No need to tell the world that you are on your honeymoon in the Bahamas—just state when you are leaving, when you are returning, and who to contact in case of emergencies.

Finally, let's talk about personal emails. Personal emails sent from the office are regarded as official company communications, regardless of content, and could possibly expose you and your company to unnecessary risk. There is nothing personal about email, no matter what you think. Email belongs to the company. The company has the right to check your emails at any time and they do not have to tell you when. If it's not something you want to defend later, don't put it in writing. That goes for venting about your boss, divulging the details about that top-secret new client, or sending off a resume to a competitor—each will land you in hot water.

To be on the safe side, always give your email a careful look before you send it into cyberspace. Is it coherent? Are there spelling errors? Does it reinforce the success brand you aim for? If so, hit send!

Texting

With the advent of cell phones and PDAs, texting has become an increasingly common way to communicate. It's quick, it's efficient and it's to the point. Unfortunately, text-messaging has also spawned an egregious lapse of proper language skills that can seriously hamper one's professional image. Read on for insight on how to stay classy while you stay connected.

To Text or Not To Text

The reason why texting has taken off is largely due to its rapid-fire efficiency. Unlike email, you don't need a computer or Internet connection, and it's generally faster than a phone call because you don't get drawn into a lengthy conversation. That said, a text message may not be the most appropriate means for your communication.

First, consider the length of your message. If what you are trying to say requires a lot of detail or explanation, call or send an email instead. Generally, messages over 150 characters belong in an email, not a text message.

You should also consider the nature of your message. Bad news—say, news of a deal or promotion that's fallen through—shouldn't be delivered via text. Soften the blow with a thoughtful phone call.

It's also important that text messages be clear and coherent. Written messages lack the subtle signals—such as a change in tone or body language—of oral communication. And because text messages are so short, they often leave plenty of room for misinterpretation. Don't rub people the wrong way with an abrupt text!

Additionally, think about the relationship you have with the person you are trying to reach. You may not think twice about texting a friend, but it implies a certain casual intimacy that may or may not be appropriate with a work colleague or boss. If you're unsure about this, wait for the person to invite you to text them, or for them to text you first. You may also ask them if it's okay to send a text if they are waiting for an urgent response from you. Keep in mind that not everyone has text message capabilities on their phone, or that they may prefer more traditional forms of communication, particularly if they're not tech-savvy.

In general, reserve texting for simple confirmations, not back-and-forth conversations that really should be documented. Messages along the lines of "I'm on my way to meet you," or, "I just received your package" are fine; calling in sick or trying to explain a complex report are not. Finally, note that some texts may not arrive immediately when you hit send. Don't just text and assume it went out. If the situation is urgent, pick up the phone.

Texting Tastefully

Phone companies may make light of text-speak, but the habit of resorting to cutesy acronyms like LOL has no place in the business world. You aren't a teenager anymore, so don't text like one. If you're pressed for time, use predictive text, a built-in service on your phone that will automatically spell out common words for you; this is faster and more efficient, but do be careful that the "predictive" word is the exact word you want to use. And resist the urge to use emoticons, such as a smiley face or a wink. They come across as immature—not professional.

You should also always proofread your text carefully before sending it, as you would with an email. Typos reflect poorly on you.

And don't forget to identify yourself at the beginning of your text. The recipient may not have your number stored in their phone contacts, so this will help avoid any confusion. Simply say, "Hi John, it's Jane from the office" before launching into your message. End your note with a "thank you" or "take care."

One more thing: avoid sending mass text messages—such as holiday greetings—to your business colleagues. A professional-looking card is more appropriate.

Playing by the Rules

Sending a clear, effective message is only part of practicing good text etiquette. You should also be considerate when you receive a text. Don't answer a text when you are in the middle of a conversation with someone else. It's as bad as taking a phone call during dinner. If you think that the message may be urgent, wait a moment, then politely excuse yourself and handle it in the restroom or lobby. The same goes for when you're at the office. Wait until you are on a break to read and respond to any personal text messages.

You'd be surprised, but I've also seen people brazenly text during a movie. Yes, it's silent, but it's incredibly rude, and the light from the phone is disrupting. Turn your phone completely off if you are going into an event requiring your full attention—whether it's a movie or a meeting. Don't try to clandestinely sneak in a text from under your desk.

Finally, do not even think of texting while driving—you'll be asking for an accident, and it is also already, or about to become, illegal in several states. Likewise, texting while walking down the street is also unwise. Multi-tasking is great, but not when it increases your risk of getting hurt.

Conclusion

Now that you know the ground rules of tech etiquette, you'll know to hold yourself to a higher standard as you do your business over text and email. These high-tech communication tools are all essential parts of building a successful personal brand in today's modern world. Make it the best brand you can. And remember: technology may come and go, but good etiquette is always in style.

PEGGY M. PARKS, AICI CIP
The Parks Image Group, Inc.

Keeping your image professional,
polished & plugged-in

(404) 266-3858
peggy@theparksimagegroup.com
www.theparksimagegroup.com

Peggy M. Parks, AICI CIP, is an international image consultant and the founder of The Parks Image Group, based in Atlanta, Georgia.

She leads corporate workshops on professional business attire and etiquette, conducts private consultations to help clients craft their personal image plan, and provides wardrobe planning and selection services.

Peggy's innate sense of style, inspired by her mother, and by a grandmother who worked in Parisian haute couture, was enhanced by studies at the London Image Institute. Peggy earned her Certified Image Professional certification in 2007.

With a corporate background in international business, Peggy has an expert sense of style and fluency in three languages—English, French and Spanish. Peggy is often featured in newspaper and magazine articles and is a frequent guest on local radio and television shows.

Peggy was a nominee for NAWBO-Atlanta's prestigious WE Shine Award and she is the 2008 recipient of the "Results Count" award from Atlanta Women in Business. Among her stellar clients, in addition to a number of professional firms, are the Southern Company, UPS and The Coca-Cola Company.

Give a Great Presentation
Effective Public Speaking for Executive Impact

By Maureen Merrill

Every executive is, sooner or later, called on to speak in front of others. Welcome these opportunities. Make the most of them. A clear message delivered with confidence creates a personal connection, persuades listeners, promotes careers and causes, and elevates the status of the speaker.

When a speech goes well, it's usually because:

- The message is clear
- The speaker is well-prepared
- The delivery is confident

Maybe there are no *bad* public speakers. However, many presentations are poorly prepared and abysmally delivered—we've all been in *that* audience. Yet almost every motivated executive and organizational leader can learn to deliver a good, solid and persuasive speech.

Confidence is the biggest issue for those who say they hate or fear public speaking. Even the clearest-thinking expert or most passionate advocate for a cause may be stunningly articulate in casual conversation, yet can stammer, lose concentration and muddle the message once he or she is on-stage, on-camera or in front of a microphone.

Would it surprise you to learn that overconfidence is also a factor when speeches go wrong? Some people seem very sure of themselves, but they're oversold on the fascination factor of their message or their delivery. They don't prepare, won't practice, and tell themselves lies. Does "I'll be fine once I'm up there" sound familiar? How about, "I perform better under the pressure of the moment," or, "I need to be spontaneous."

No one expects to dance a ballet, argue a case before a judge, draw a portrait, or throw a perfect pass on a football field without study, training and practice. Many organizational leaders, who are generally smart, articulate folks, think they "should" be good speakers without much effort. Yet, naturally able speakers are rare. Most of us, after a speech, feel that we could have done better. We need to give as much time and attention to speaking as we do to our wardrobes, the reports we write, and the projects we plan.

Let's look at three major factors of speaking well in public:

• Message

• Preparation

• Delivery

Typically, speakers have far more to say than time allows. When we're passionate about a subject and determined to explain why it matters, the history behind it, what we want people to do or believe and how the future will be different because . . . well, we could go on and on. The trouble is, we often do just that.

The further trouble is that listeners will only remember brief bits of what we say. We might reason if we give listeners a whole lot of information, we increase the chance that some of it sticks. Sadly, the opposite occurs. The more we say, the less people will remember.

So we have to get to the essence of the message. We must leave much out if we wish to convey anything. Mark Twain knew that this wasn't easy. "If you want me to give you a two-hour presentation," he said, "I am ready today. If you want only a five-minute speech, it will take me two weeks to prepare." To effectively hone down a message, begin with the end in mind.

Decide What You Want To Accomplish With Your Talk

When it's all over and people are walking out, what do you want them to do, remember or believe? What impression do you want to make?

For example, a possible outcome of your talk could be that listeners:

- Embrace a cause or adopt a point of view
- Take an action; for example, buy your product or service, join your organization, or make a donation
- Learn something, enjoy themselves, or be entertained
- View you as a credible and confident leader, or as an expert
- Appreciate your star quality, or get to know and like you

Identify What's In It For Your Listeners

Be very clear about why your audience should care. People remember that which they care about. They care about what they can connect with, and that includes the messenger. Several touchpoints can connect you, the speaker to each member of your audience on a personal level:

- Immediate impacts on one's life, such as prices, taxes, breathable air, crime, overcrowding or traffic.
- Issues that most people care deeply about, such as the well-being of children, war, health, justice, gang violence, or the environment.
- The nearly universal desire to help others, improve the human condition, leave a legacy, or make a better world.
- Quality of life matters such as vitality, personal effectiveness, social and business success, rich cultural experiences; the appeal of laughing, having fun, being entertained, and learning.

Too many presentations are speaker-centered, based on the speaker's agenda; the audience is treated as passive receptors. To connect with what your audience cares about, to make it worth their time to listen to you, you must know your audience. That said, there's no such thing as "talking to an audience." You are talking to individuals who happen to be sitting in a group. Keep in mind that your message is being heard—one person at a time.

Preparation

1. Clarify the main, paramount point of your presentation. Examples:

- Our firm is the best at what we do.

- I will make an excellent governor of this state.

- Embrace my vision for how our company should become involved in the community.

- Reducing your carbon footprint leads to happiness.

2. Define two or three sub-points, or supporting points that you want to make. Sub-points can be:

- **Evidence,** such as: "Our professional services are used by successful companies." "A gang member turned his life around, thanks to our program." "This is the experience that qualifies me to lead."

- **Arguments** on the cause or philosophy that you wish to promote: "Sexual harassment degrades our corporate culture, polluting the work environment through offensive, illegal and inappropriate behavior."

- **Pieces of new information:** "Here's how to reduce landfill garbage and why it's easier than you think."

For each sub-point, add:

- One or two specific examples
- One or two "swirls"—human interest anecdotes, humor, touching references to people, or quotes.

Make your "swirls" specific and human; use names and describe situations in vivid terms. "John is a thin, blond-haired boy, once astonishing in his speed and grace on a skateboard. He's now weak, blank-eyed and losing his teeth. He's been on crystal meth for six months."

Your major point and the sub-points now comprise the three- or four-part body of your talk.

Choose A Beginning Thought And An Ending Thought.

The opening of your talk should get attention, assure audience members that they're in good hands with you, and give them some idea of why they should listen. It might be a shocking statistic, a story about a client, or a provocative idea that can't help but get the audience to wondering what you've got to say.

Compose an ending that underscores the main intention for the talk that contains or repeats a strong idea related to your message, and ends on a note of your choice: bright, solemn, moving or funny. Quotes can work very well.

Should You Use Notes?

I would like you to be so familiar with your topic that you use very few—preferably no—notes in a short presentation, for example, to a civic or networking group. When you give a seminar or lead a workshop, you likely will need notes, and you may insist on using them in any situation. In any case, notes are just that; they're not whole sentences and paragraphs. Marking off certain areas with a colored felt pen will help you find your place as you move along.

Delivery—How to Practice

First generate the words that will present the message you've constructed. This is not exactly the same as saying, "Write your speech." At first, just go through your message in your own words, part by part, out loud, as if you were explaining it all to a very interested friend. Don't stop to correct yourself or improve. Repeat this process, and time yourself during the second run-through. You'll likely find that some pieces don't work. You may revisit the order of your points, the supporting ideas, and the "swirls." Notice which parts flow freely, and which don't.

Now, for the most important phase of your practice, give your presentation on video. Except for professional coaching, this is the most valuable feedback you can get. It is even more valuable if you can record yourself practicing the speech in front of one or two people.

Listen to your voice. Do you end many sentences or phrases with a questioning tone? Do you have a "like" or "you know" habit? Is your voice tentative? Harsh?

Check for fidgeting, "waltzing" in place, or shifting your weight back and forth. Many speakers rest their weight on one leg, which pokes one hip out and makes for poor posture. Plant your feet squarely on the ground.

What They See Is What They Get

Call to mind a speaker you've heard recently. Chances are, you've got a visual in your head right now, because the first thing you did was to picture the person. This visual memory is far stronger than your memory of how the person sounded—which is probably the second thing you remember—and what the person said. If the speaker did a good job, or if the topic was important to you, you may remember details, perhaps a repeated phrase or two, or a story or point that resonated. You also remember whether you enjoyed the speaker, and whether you'd want to hear that person again.

Your own speech works the same way. People will grant you credibility, and judge your ideas, based mainly on what they see, how you sound and how they reacted. The extent to which that works will determine whether your delivery was effective.

Does that mean that what you say isn't important? Not at all. Without good, well-organized material—also known as "something to say"—you won't come across as assured or confident. When your look and sound don't connect, you have to work much harder to get your content across.

When deciding what to wear for a presentation, ask this: does my appearance show respect for the audience? In most business situations, a suit shows respect. Even in the high-tech industry, which supposedly brought us the dubious gift of sweats-and-tennies workwear, official website photos of company leaders (for example, at Microsoft, Oracle and Sun Microsystems) show the great majority wearing suits. Those few not in suits wear collared shirts or neat sweaters.

Most professional speakers follow this rule of thumb: dress one level up from the audience. This isn't you trying to look better than them. It's you showing respect, by presenting yourself at your best, consistent with dressing appropriately to the environment. In most civic and business situations, a suit is a safe and credible choice. If you're at a weekend retreat and everyone's in jeans, maybe you wear slacks or add a casual blazer.

Visual Aids and PowerPoint Pitfalls

Most presentations are improved by some visual aids, which can be as simple as photographs, a model of what you're talking about, or even a book that you hold up.

PowerPoint can be great if you're leading a seminar or workshop, especially if you want to show photos or charts. But if you are talking to a small group or civic organization, you probably don't need it. A couple of posters or flip charts, especially for small groups, will generally give you enough visual back-up for your main points.

Don't use PowerPoint when your main purpose is to underscore your status as a leader. Don't use it when your primary purpose is to inspire, rather than inform.

If you do determine that the judicious use of PowerPoint is called for—beware. Jaded audiences have reached a point of fatigue with PowerPoint abuse and over-use. Follow these guidelines:

• Simple, simple, simple. No swooping paragraphs or bouncing words. Each slide should have the same general look and feel, even if you use varied colors.

• Use as few words as possible. Many slides are overloaded with words. Remember: the more information presented, the less retained.

• Never read your slides. Your audience will finish reading long before you do, and they'll be murmuring among themselves or mentally drawing up "To-Do" lists while you drone on.

• Projectors these days are strong enough for normal room light. Dim lights encourage napping.

• Don't use the PowerPoint presentation as a substitute for notes. This disconnects you from the audience, as you're always checking with the screen.

• Don't turn your back or your side to the audience to look at your PowerPoint slides.

Is it Okay to Read a Speech?

No—ideally, no. Sometimes, such as at a large convention where your remarks may be not only transcribed but simultaneously translated, you may need to stick to a verbatim speech. These venues usually provide invisible-to-the-audience reading equipment that lets you keep eye contact and avoid reading from paper at the podium.

Unfortunately, there are occasions when a speaker simply doesn't take the time to develop a speech, or sharpen his or her delivery skills. I recently heard the highly educated president of a major national news organization read an entire 35-minute keynote, seldom looking up. She conveyed some interesting information, but she didn't come across as a leader.

If you must read a speech, use these pointers to make it work better:

• Add notes or symbols to remind yourself to look up, make eye contact and smile frequently. Mark these spots with color so that you'll immediately know where to resume reading again.

• Go through the whole speech a dozen or more times out loud, ahead of time. As you once may have done in grade school with the Gettysburg Address, you'll end up learning large parts of your text in spite of yourself.

• Don't apologize for reading.

• Learn your final few phrases so that you don't have to read them.

"And in Conclusion . . ."

Although it's considered the most common and greatest human fear, public speaking is not at all a strange activity. After all, unless we're talking to ourselves in the shower or the car, isn't all speaking public speaking?

Every leader wants to communicate well, and all good communicators want to become great communicators. Speaking skills give us an edge over competitors, increase credibility, raise our profiles and inspire confidence in others.

Because communication is at the essence of leadership, and of helping and developing others, it deserves our energy and our best attention. Don't expect perfection, but do go for excellence. Stay "in training" as a speaker; practice diligently, learn from other speakers and always seek fresh and creative ways to express yourself.

MAUREEN MERRILL
Harris Merrill Communication Consulting

Communication is the
essential business tool

(707) 544-7286
maureen@harrismerrill.com
www.harrismerrill.com

Maureen McDaniel Merrill has helped many business and professional leaders develop superb skills in self-expression and presentation. Through individual sessions and lively workshops, Harris Merrill Speech Coaching prepares clients for interviews, public addresses, media appearances and presentations to small and large groups.

Because every speaker and every audience is unique, Harris Merrill works with the individual strengths of each client. We start with the end in mind, clarifying personal goals and the purposes of upcoming presentations. Maureen's special talent is in helping clients develop authentic, powerful messages, and to deliver them in a natural, engaging and persuasive manner. In her clients' words:

"The impact was significant and immediate."
—Newspaper publisher

"She is energetic, knowledgeable, articulate, funny and a dynamic and skillful presenter . . . In one word, she's a winner!"
—School district superintendent

"Two thumbs up!"—Sports psychologist/motivational speaker

Maureen holds an MA in Psychology from San Francisco State University and is a former elected city council member. She is a popular speaker and leadership consultant in Rotary International, and has served on several civic and charitable boards.

Make It Your Best "15 Minutes"

Looking Your Best for Television, Video and Videoconferencing

By Suzanne Mauro, AICI FLC

The saying "Everyone will be famous for 15 minutes," made infamous by the painter Andy Warhol in 1968, is something I tell all my clients. Being ready for a TV appearance, a videoconference meeting, a webcast, or a video taping for a media outlet can be very exciting. You will probably spend many hours carefully choosing what you will say or do. Chances are, you will also spend endless hours deciding what to wear. If you appear in the media, you need to make a good impression immediately or risk losing your audience.

In my professional life, I have worked with on-air talent in all forms of media to show them how to look their very best. I have tackled endless wardrobe issues, pulling rabbits out of my cliché hats to make everything come together before the camera starts rolling. When it comes to media, your look is such an important part of the package; that's why celebrities have stylists who spend hours creating their best look, from head to toe. When I begin to work with on-air talent, I start by figuring out what works for them and what doesn't. Remember, how you look definitely affects how you are perceived by your audience.

When you have an important TV, webcast or videoconferencing appearance coming up, consider working with a good media stylist. That way, you will be confident in your appearance and able to relax. Until then, or even if you do have a stylist, there is a lot for you to know to be effective on the air, via the web, or on the big screen in the conference room.

Follow the advice in this chapter to make sure you give the impression you intend in all media, whether your audience is made up of hundreds of thousands of TV viewers, or one CEO in a boardroom across the globe.

Your Mother is Your Best Critic

The best compliment I ever received was when the mother of one of my on-air clients said, "My daughter never looked so good as when you dressed her." I take this to heart, because I know moms make the best critics. Mine always did.

In this day and age, especially with high-definition television (HDTV), you have to be camera-ready. TV cameras have X-ray eyes. Today's lenses are greatly enhanced and see more than the eye can see. Start by doing your homework and gather enough information that will enable you to look and feel your best when the television or video camera is trained on you.

Find out as much as you can about the surroundings of the studio or on-location shoot, especially the background color of the set. You don't want your clothing to blend in and make you invisible.

Ask the producer or your booking agent if there are any colors you should avoid. Even if you are giving a speech to a large audience and your presentation will be displayed on projection screens, it is crucial to know the background color. If you are wearing a dark blue suit and the velvet curtains behind you are dark blue, you will look like a talking head on the projection screens, and your audience will be too distracted to hear a word you say.

Will you be sitting or standing? Will your entire body be in the frame, or just your face, shoulders and upper torso? Will you be shooting indoors or outside? What will the other people on the set be wearing? After all, you never want to be overdressed or underdressed.

Television studios are kept cool to negate the effect of the hot lights. Yet everyone who has ever appeared on television has felt nervous at one time or another, including famous people. Consider dress shields if you perspire easily, and bring a handkerchief or tissue to dab your face during breaks.

Getting Ready for the Camera

Remember, for TV you will need to be miked, so make sure that a lapel microphone and transmitter can be easily attached to your clothing. Shirt, dress, sweater and blazer collars work well. Turtlenecks and collarless shirts can be challenging, and fragile knits can be damaged by a microphone clip. The best placement for a microphone clip is about five inches below the chin, or about two shirt buttons from the top.

When the camera is on you, be conscious of your body language, tone of voice and facial movement. See Beverly Samuel's chapter on *The Nine Tenets of Body Language* on page 127 for more on this important topic.

Practice good posture. Sit or stand leaning slightly forward, with legs crossed at the ankles, or one foot slightly in front of the other, if you are standing. Keep your posture erect; this helps slenderize and elongate your frame.

When sitting, do not cross your legs at the knees. It becomes easy to unconsciously bounce your foot and also, the soles of your shoes will show. Both can be distracting.

Try to tape your appearance, or ask the producer for a copy of the video tape. Study it later as a learning tool, to be your own best critic. Most people do not like what they see the first time they see themselves on video. That's all the more reason to watch yourself and get past your initial displeasure so you can be objective and pay attention to ways you can do better the next time.

Avoid too-large, dangly or shiny jewelry that may conflict with lighting and sound. Anything that outshines or out-sparkles your eyes or face is not a good choice.

Color is Powerful

I can still remember observing my first on-air client. Our color choice made such an amazing impact on how she looked on-air. Color can be used as a powerful tool that can give you fabulous results and make your face the center of attention—not your outfit. When you look at your wardrobe and try to decide what to wear, view the article from the standpoint of how vibrant its color or pattern is. When you are appearing on TV, you are dealing with high-powered lenses that have difficulty balancing certain colors. Example of some color extremes: black, white or red. Definitely avoid fabric patterns that might shimmer or vibrate on TV cameras, such as stripes, polka-dots, iridescent, checked or multicolored fabrics. Dark colors absorb the light and make you look smaller. Light colors reflect the light and make you look larger. A good tip: try to stay in the center of the color spectrum.

Blue and purple. Blue is the most pleasant color of all, because it is in the middle of the spectrum. Try a deep blue suit with either a blouse matched in color to the suit or in a muted, jewel tone. Good blue variations are navy, royal blue, marine blue, French blue, cadet blue or a slate-gray blue. Periwinkle blue or non-bright aquas work as well. Purples with red tones and plum shades are flattering colors.

Green. Stay away from bright greens and kelly greens. Jade green, dark emerald and soft olive greens, however, are fabulous.

Red. Red does signify confidence, leadership and independence, but your clothing will be seen before you are. Red can also reflect on the whites of your eyes and cast heat onto your skin tone.

Orange. Terra cotta, apricot, brick and autumn leaf tones are good middle-spectrum colors. Stay away from bright orange and yellow, which can be harsh and unbecoming to all skin tones.

Brown. Brown should not be your primary choice. Taupe, rust or clay are great neutral colors.

Gray. Gray flatters you and makes a statement of strength. It denotes confidence, success and trustworthiness. Good variations are slate gray, dove gray, charcoal gray, steel gray and oxford gray. Gray is compatible with many other colors and is easily accessorized.

White. White makes everything look larger. A white dress or skirt will add pounds to your image. If you can look at a TV monitor, you will see that a white blouse or jacket looks larger than it really is.

Black. Black can appear harsh against most skin tones. For a woman whose face is starting to show her age, black can make the face look even older.

Don't be afraid to approach local retailers to see if you can borrow an outfit for your on-air appearance. If you give them a plug for their clothing, it is a great media trade and they will love the free publicity.

Camera-Ready

When you find the perfect outfit, photograph yourself from top to bottom in a full-length mirror. Look at yourself from the sides, front, and back. Make sure it is your best choice. Good fit is essential, so better a little roomy than too tight. Tight clothes that pull across the front will make you look heavier. A tight skirt will hike above the knees and wrinkle across the front if you have to sit down. You should have at least an inch of leeway in the fabric on each side of your hips.

You must feel comfortable in your clothes. Never wear a new outfit for the first time in front of your audience. You need to know in advance how the whole outfit looks when you are standing, sitting or moving about. You need to forget about what you are wearing and concentrate on what you are saying.

Bare arms attract the eye away from the face, because they are lighter in color. You might want to consider wearing long sleeves, which will slenderize your silhouette and look more professional.

Your neckline should conform to the contours of your face. You can lengthen your face with a V neckline or use a scarf to soften the effect. If you have a short neck, avoid bows, turtlenecks and high collars.

If you are like me and have a tendency to gesture with your hands, they must look good without attracting too much attention away from your face. To make fingers look longer, taper the nails slightly and use a clear, pink-tinged, or flesh-colored polish. Long fingernails with bright or dark polish cut off the ends of the fingers and attract too much attention. Always direct your gestures towards your interviewer, and remember that all gestures on camera look magnified. High gestures reveal tension, and wide gestures look wild. While gesturing is fine on-air, it is important to note that you want to sit still and keep your head and shoulders steady. Remember, you have to stay within the frame of the camera. If you are moving around too much, the camera may not be able to stay with you.

Ask any good stylist and they will tell you that the most important part of dressing is the undergarment. I highly recommend a great shapewear foundation, because it will cinch your waist, eliminate any midriff, back roll, and panty lines. A smoother clothing line always looks best on-camera.

When you are going to be on television, it is always good to bring a change of clothes. This could be a really smart idea if your original choice turns out to be the exact same color as the wall behind you.

A Girl Can't Live on Clothes Alone—Accessories Are Essential

When I show up for a shoot, I always bring tons of accessories, because I believe that is the secret to making basic clothes look good. An accessory can make the smallest difference, and enhance your appearance on-screen. The basic rule for television and video is that anything that sparkles or shines too much, dangles in the light, or rattles and makes noise will distract attention from your face and what you are saying. Better jewelry choices are:

Pearls, even colored ones. Sixteen-inch single strands have serious finishing power; layer lengths for a funkier approach.

Beads in subdued, rich colors. If you like bold bead necklaces, consider matching the color of your top to the necklace.

These ideas will not overpower your total look, and work well for HDTV: colored, semiprecious stones set in pins, earrings and necklaces; amethyst, garnet and dark-blue topaz; rich, jewel-tone colors like deep purple.

The Perfect Male

My male clients' clothing needs are very basic: comfortable, naturals for mixing and matching, and easy to clean, but most important, men want to look awesome! Here are some helpful guidelines for a suitable media appearance:

Stay away from bold pattern suits, plaids, checks, stripes or garish colors. When sitting, unbutton the bottom button of your suit jacket for a smoother look in your shoulder. Forget company logo shirts, which have a tendency to be boxy on-camera, and get lost in close-range shots. A grey shirt is the most flattering neutral color; it is soft and works well with camera lights. Stay away from white shirts because they dominate on-camera and will appear brighter than your face.

Avoid bold pattern neckties, polka dots, stripes, plaids, and shiny fabric. Your necktie should enhance the color of your eyes. Try for a middle-spectrum color. A perfect tie knot is between $2\frac{1}{4}$ and $3\frac{1}{4}$ inches for the widest part of the tie, and from $1\frac{1}{2}$ to $1\frac{3}{4}$ inches across the thickest part of the knot. Anything larger will look too hefty under your chin. Be careful with jewelry; large watches, cufflinks, lapel pins or large rings may flash light into the camera as you move.

Videoconferencing

Everything we have just discussed for your TV appearances also applies to participating in webcasts, videoconferencing, even talking to a business associate or client via your webcam.

One more challenge to be aware of when conducting business or presenting via a webcast, webcam or videoconference: stay still and avoid gesturing when working in this medium. Here's why. The constant stream of dots-per-inch that is being transmitted stays constant when you are only moving your mouth. If you are jumpy or gesture quickly, the image that appears on the monitor or screen of your viewer has to be built again from scratch. This means your audio will be uninterrupted, but your picture on monitors and screens will be delayed, which can get very frustrating for your viewers.

Be Ready for Any Emergency

The Boy Scouts® were right—always be prepared—especially when the world is watching. Assemble a kit for emergency situations. Set up a lunch box or tool box-size arsenal that has you well-prepared for every conceivable situation you might find yourself in, even at the most inopportune time. Bad hair day? No problem—you have spray and gel. Spot on your lapel? No problem—you have a brooch or handkerchief ready as camouflage. Fill your kit with spot remover, static guard, a lint brush, safety pins, dress shields, hairpins, an extra pair of hose, and extra makeup.

Follow my professional advice to meet the challenges you will face as an executive in the public eye, and your experiences in front of the camera will be successful. I have one final piece of advice, perhaps the most important: be yourself, and have fun. That's when we're all at our personal best.

SUZANNE MAURO, AICI FLC
Stylist and Image Consultant

Style every day

(412) 537-4735
suz@suzannemauro.com
www.suzannemauro.com

Suzanne Mauro is a fashionistering stylist who has been helping men and women look and feel more beautiful for over three decades. She has worked with television and entertainment personalities as well as with business individuals and organizations such as *The Jennifer TV Show,* KDKA-TV news anchors (Pittsburgh), and Dress for Success.

She is a certified professional stylist and image consultant for Nordstrom and themodernmatchmaker.com, a national professional matchmaking service. Suzanne also contributes her talents and time to Divabetics, adding fashion-friendly workshops and education support for divas with diabetes to her stylish routine. Additional positions have included on-air fashion editor, fashion coordinator, modeling/acting teacher and mentor for fashion teen boards. Fashion editorial spreads, commercials, fashion shows and production roles complete her portfolio.

Suzanne is a Pisces and resides in Pittsburgh, Pennsylvania, with her three fashionable cats, and her many, many accessories.

China
How to Succeed in the 21st Century's Gold Rush
By Betty Chu, AICI FLC

In a rapidly expanding global economy, China is the 21st century's "Gold Rush" for business. Companies in almost every industry flock to China to stake their claims. Knowing the cultural differences, and mastering Chinese etiquette and protocol skills, can give you a distinct advantage over your competition. You will project the image of a polished, world-class executive, which can help you to successfully promote or conduct business with Chinese executives.

Why Learning Chinese Customs and Etiquette is Important

China will be the largest economy in the world. According to the forecasts of the Goldman Sachs economists at the World Bank, and numerous editorials in the New York Times, Time magazine, USA Today and on BBC News, economists have reached a consensus. China is set to become the world's largest economy within two decades.

China is only the beginning. Despite the geographical and political differences, in a cultural and economic sense, the greater China region includes not only the People's Republic of China, but also three out of the "Four Tigers" of Asia: Hong Kong—an entrepreneurial center; Taiwan—a technologically advanced island, the world's largest producer of notebook computers; and predominantly Chinese (76.7 percent) Singapore, a base for many multinational enterprises.

China's influence on its neighbors. The Chinese business elite of Southeast Asia who live in Malaysia, Indonesia, Vietnam, Thailand, the Philippines, and South Korea, all share the same cultural values.

Human resources. China is the most populous nation in the world (more than 1.3 billion people), plus over 30 million Chinese live in neighboring Southeast Asia. This group includes many business owners, highly educated professionals, engineers, and seasoned import-export executives, all of whom represent unequaled potential.

The Chinese diaspora. An estimated 12 million Chinese live in the United States, Canada, Australia, Europe and Latin America. Many global business-savvy Chinese pay homage to their cultural tradition by investing back in their homeland and endowing the universities that educated them.

Capital. Together, China, Taiwan, Hong Kong and Singapore have three-quarters of a trillion dollars in foreign reserves. With its tremendous bargaining power, this area is becoming more and more prominent in international business. World affairs will soon no longer be dominated only by America and Europe.

The world's factory (export power). China is no longer only the supplier of labor. Today, complex products such as electronic toys, bicycles, and designer clothing are manufactured in China, which is also a dominant global player in home appliances. China-made components are used extensively by all industries worldwide.

World's largest marketplace (import power). With more than 1.3 billion consumers, China is the most attractive market for foreign products and corporations. For example, it is already the largest market for commercial aircraft and machine tool makers, and the most promising automotive market in the world.

Job opportunities. The huge Chinese market is creating jobs for the industries that export their goods and services to China. Chinese investment is also creating jobs by building roads and railways, opening textile factories, and digging oil wells in countries such as Africa and Brazil.

Chinese Society and Culture: Some Differences

The world is changing so rapidly through globalization that understanding cultural differences is simultaneously vital and beneficial.

High context culture. Chinese culture is shaped by thousands of years of history. Despite the changes of the political environment in the recent one hundred years, the same cultural values and customs are shared by more than 1.35 billion Chinese all over the world. According to the terms presented by anthropologist Edward T. Hall (*Beyond Culture,* Anchor Books, New York, 1976) decades ago, the Chinese culture is a high context culture. Some of the characteristics are:

- People have a strong sense of tradition and history, and change little over time. In contrast, low context cultures change drastically from one generation to the next, like in the United States, German-speaking countries, Scandinavian countries and France, where the individual is valued over the group.

- Many things are left unsaid and expected to be explained by culture itself or implicitly understood instead of explained through words or verbalization as in low context cultures.

Confucianism

Confucianism is a complex system of moral, social, political, and philosophical thought that has had tremendous influence on the Chinese culture. It stresses duty, sincerity, loyalty, honor, filial piety, respect for age and seniority and teaches that a harmonious world results from every individual playing his or her part well in the social order, and that maintaining harmonious families leads to a stable society and peaceful world.

The Importance of "Face"

"Face" *(pronounced mian-zi)* is vitally important to the Chinese. To cause someone to lose face by showing disrespect or public humiliation will cost you the deal, and maybe even the opportunity to do business with others. On the other hand, by doing something to enhance someone's image or reputation, or being generous in gift giving or entertaining your guests is to give that person "face."

"Face" roughly translates as "honor" or "respect." It is an abstract concept, but Chinese are very sensitive to how they are regarded by others. Groups and organizations have face, too; schools, corporations and bureaus all have reputations to worry about.

It is critical that you avoid losing face or cause the loss of face at all times. A few examples of causing someone to lose face are:

- Talking down or insulting a person in front of one's peers.
- Failing to show proper respect to a person.
- Rejecting a sincere request or plea for help.
- Failing or being defeated in competitions.

The Importance of Interpersonal Relationships

"Guan-xi" translates to "connections or networking." This normally means doing favors for someone you know. For centuries, Chinese have relied on their "trusted networks" to find jobs, spouses, good schools for their children or customers for their businesses. They feel morally obligated to help each member of their group: their extended family, workplace, school or people sharing the same social experiences, even people having the same last name.

Since these "ties" or "kinships" are very important to the Chinese, they prefer to do business with an "old friend" from the network, instead of with a total stranger. Being introduced by a trusted intermediary can help build trust and the "old friend" status can be attained rapidly.

Collectivism Versus Individualism—
The Fundamental Difference Between Chinese and Westerners

While western people embrace personal achievement, individuality, creativity and independence, the Chinese view individuality as not as important as group membership. It is a collective society; children are taught that they are members of a group. One's actions reflect not only on oneself, but on the group (family, school, companies or even country). Some key points to consider are:

- It is important to the Chinese to act with decorum at all times.

- Chinese individuals will not do anything to cause embarrassment to their group.

- Most Chinese people will subjugate their own feelings for the good of the group.

- Chinese will submit to authority more willingly than westerners.

- Matters are often debated until a consensus is reached; after that, members are expected to follow and act without question.

Nonverbal Communication

Facial expression. Most Chinese maintain an impassive expression when speaking. Since modesty is a highly valued trait, the Chinese will not display overexcited gestures or emotions over achievements or victories.

Personal space. Due to the density of the population, Chinese are comfortable with less personal space, yet they are not comfortable staring into another person's eyes, especially those of the opposite sex, and often avoid eye contact in a crowded place.

Body language and physical contact. Traditionally, older or more conservative Chinese are seldom demonstrative with the opposite sex in public. Touching, hugging or other types of physical contact with the opposite sex, elders and high-ranking officials should be avoided. In general, Chinese are more comfortable if people of the same sex have physical contact in public. Young ladies holding hands or leaning on a friend walking down the street are common; that is nothing more than showing the affection of the friendship. If you ask a question to a Chinese person, he or she may smile or laugh instead of answering. That could mean the person needs to consult with someone privately before the final answer can be given. "No" can be expressed in many subtle ways, such as sucking in air through clenched teeth, or saying "It's inconvenient," or "We are still considering your proposal."

Hierarchical Society

In China, all organizations, whether private or government, are hierarchical, with well-defined ranks and authorities. Decisions are made from the top down.

Customs and Etiquettes

Meeting and Greeting Etiquette. Business meetings are usually held in conference rooms, rather than in offices or restaurants.

- Always be punctual; arriving late is an insult and could negatively affect your relationship.

- Greetings are formal, and the oldest person is always greeted first.

- Handshakes are the most common form of greeting with foreigners.

- Many Chinese are less comfortable with eye contact and will look toward the ground when greeting someone.

- Guests are usually greeted by lower-ranking representatives, then escorted to the conference room.

- Since Chinese do not like surprises, you should send an agenda, and supply information about your company and what you want to accomplish at the meeting in advance.

- Officials or senior officers are always accompanied by staff members at a meeting; it is important to know who is the decision maker. Generally, whoever enters the door first is the boss, and those who are not introduced are staff.

- Building relationships is important, so begin with small talk, break the ice, and don't dive into discussing business issues right away.

- Don't insist on your position at the meeting; leave room for further discussion.

- Chinese executives usually send representatives to the airport to greet and welcome foreign visitors, and also see them off at the conclusion of business. If you host Chinese executives abroad, be sure to extend the same airport rituals, as you will score extra points and solidify your business relationship.

Name and title. Names are very important to the Chinese; you must know how to address someone properly when you first meet.

- Chinese naming order: family name first and given name second.

- The Chinese given name is unique and has profound meanings; some names bear the generation character, and most symbolize the expectations or best wishes from the parents or grandparents into one or two, out of over 50,000 Chinese characters. It is unlikely to see the same given names in a class or workplace.

- It is not respectful to call parents, elders or senior officers by their first name, or their full names.

- In business, it is recommended that you call a Chinese person by the honorific title plus the last name, such as Director Chen, Manager Lin or even Miss Wong. You may also drop the last name altogether, just call the person by their title to show your respect, such as General Manager, Principal, Teacher.

- In social settings, or even among friends and family, Chinese children are taught to call family friends "Uncle + last name" for a male, and "Aunt + last name" for a female, to show respect, for example, "Uncle Lee."

Business cards. Business cards should be presented with both hands, and with the name facing the receiver of the card.

Dining Etiquette

Table Manners. Practice these behaviors before dining with the Chinese:

- The host begins eating first, and offers the first toast.
- Learn how to use chopsticks; Chinese specially appreciate foreigners' sincere attempts to learn how to maneuver chopsticks.
- You should try everything that is offered to you, or explain the reasons for refusal.
- Hold the rice bowl close to your mouth while eating.
- Do not handle the food with fingers; use chopsticks.
- Do not be offended if a Chinese person makes slurping or belching sounds; that merely indicates that they are enjoying their food.
- If there is no serving spoon on the plate, turn the chopsticks around, and use the chopstick heads to serve yourself.
- Never eat the last piece from your plate.

Business Dining. Chinese prefer to entertain business guests in restaurants.

- Most savvy Chinese businesspeople, especially in Beijing, Shanghai, Hong Kong, Taipei and Singapore, have a global palate and will not serve anything "too exotic" to foreign guests.

- It is common to have people who are not involved in your business deal show up as dinner guests.

- Wait to be told where to sit. The guest of honor is usually seated facing the door.

- Gauge your appetite; you can determine how many courses will be served by the number of guests. The Chinese like even numbers; it is common to have 10 or 12 people sit around a big, round table, and that means 10 to 12 courses, so be advised you are in for a lengthy banquet.

Home Dining. If you are invited to a private house, consider it a great honor. If you must turn down such an honor, you must give an explanation, otherwise the host will "lose face."

- Arrive on time.

- Remove your shoes before entering the house.

- Bring a small gift to the hostess or children of the family; you will score high points.

- Be sure to demonstrate that you thoroughly enjoy the food.

What to Wear

- Chinese people are more formal in business settings; business attire is usually conservative and unpretentious.

- Men should wear dark conservative business suits with modest ties.

- Women should wear conservative business suits or dresses with a high neckline. Cleavage is an absolute "no-no" in both social and business settings.

- Women should wear low heels.

- Linen suits or dresses in natural color (hemp-like) should be avoided, since that color is associated with funerals.

- Red is a lucky color. If you are invited to a celebration banquet, such as a birthday, wedding, or Chinese New Year banquet, do not wear black. If you only have a black suit, wear accessories in red (tie, pocket handkerchief, scarf, or earrings) to counter the unlucky black color.

Gift Giving and Receiving Etiquette

- The visiting party is expected to give a gift to the hosting organization.

- Gifts to individuals should be small or practical.

- Scissors, knives or other cutting utensils are not good gift items, as they indicate the severing of the relationship.

- Clocks, handkerchiefs or straw sandals are associated with funerals and death.

- Do not wrap gifts in white or black paper.

- "Four" is the homonym of "death" in Mandarin Chinese. Eight is the luckiest number, so giving eight of something brings luck to the recipient.

- Always present your gifts with both hands.

- Chinese do not open gifts in front of the givers.

- It is acceptable for foreigners to open a gift when it is given.

- Learn some auspicious symbols commonly presented on Chinese gift items. Show your appreciation of the meaning of the gift; you will score extra high points with your host.

Common Auspicious Symbols

* Peony represents prosperity.
* Pine trees, cranes and turtles represent longevity.
* Cod represents success, advancing in life.
* Goldfish represents gold, wealth.
* A phoenix is the symbol of empress; a dragon is the symbol of emperor. Together, the two symbolize a "good marriage."
* Horse represents success.

Holidays

In China and the Greater China Region, there are many public holidays. The most important, celebrated by all Chinese, is the Chinese Lunar New Year, also called "Spring Festival" (varying dates—either at the end of January or in February). Avoid travel to Asia just before or during this festive period, as private or governmental organizations will be closed for at least three days.

Conclusion

In today's multicultural business world, China is a key player. One can no longer be complacent and limited; learning Chinese customs and etiquette is an important strategy in your quest to expand your prosperity and success in the international arena. The Chinese appreciate the gesture of your sincere attempt to learn a little of their language, and understand the way they do business and how they view a situation. These efforts will make them feel comfortable with you and they will want to do business with you instead of your competition.

BETTY CHU, AICI FLC
Class In Style

Succeed and prosper in the international business arena!

(408) 402-3420
betty@classinstyle.com
www.classinstyle.com

People who do business internationally often find themselves perplexed by some business and social interactions. Even sophisticated, longtime international travelers can find themselves in situations where they are at a disadvantage. Expert Betty Chu helps Asian and North American business people excel while seeking opportunities in one or both of these two world economies.

Betty Chu is a uniquely qualified image and international etiquette consultant. She was born and raised in Taipei, Taiwan, and spent the second half of her life in the United States—much of it in Silicon Valley, in the San Francisco Bay Area. She became an image consultant after a long career in art and design that included owning her own apparel company. Her particular combination of experience makes it possible to help business people master how to "dress for success," as well as what to say and do in a variety of cross-cultural business and social situations. She is a certified corporate etiquette and international protocol consultant, and was trained by the prestigious Washington School of Protocol. She has also received advanced image consultant training in both Asia and United States, and is a Certified Universal Style™ Consultant.

Betty Chu is a consummate professional—knowledgeable and sincere!

Civility
A Solid Foundation for Your Image
By Yasmin Anderson-Smith, MCRP, AICI FLC

"**T**reat your package the way you want to be treated." I was amazed to hear this profound statement made by a Post Office employee in reply to a customer's question about whether a small box was suitably wrapped for mailing abroad. There was no sarcasm in his reply, only sincerity and a certain pride as he expertly examined the package. Noting that it was secured with hospital tape, he explained that because the packaging was not secure, the box might not reach its international destination intact. The customer accepted his instructions with grace. The employee's behavior and communication reflected the true spirit of civility by demonstrating care, concern and thoughtfulness. His brief relationship with the customer was positive, productive, and smooth.

Civility Defined

Exactly what is civility? Is it important or relevant for your business image or personal brand? Civility involves how we treat others, whether we are polite and courteous. Stephen Carter's book, *Manners, Morals and the Etiquette of Democracy* (Harper Perennial Press, 1998) states that civility ". . . suggests an approach to life . . . a way of carrying one's self and relating to others." The word civility is rooted in the Latin word, civitas, meaning city, and civilité, which is a French word typically meaning politeness. Civilité also shares a common linguistic root with the words city and civilization for "member of household." This suggests that acting with civility means recognizing that one is part of a society, company, organization, community or household. The word civility involves caring about others, being concerned for their well-being, and having a sense of community, neighborly good will, and citizenship. Civility is behavior guided by rules of conduct.

Civility embraces ethics, character, attitude, esthetics and giving. Workplace attire and body language, branding, marketing, advertising, public relations, verbal, print and electronic communications are all ways in which we relate to each other. The receptionist who maintains her composure with a hostile customer, the client who brings all the necessary documents to a scheduled meeting, or the manager who observes and respects the dining etiquette of her international clients at a business luncheon, are all examples of civility in action.

Dr. P.M. Forni proposes a new way of looking at civility in his book *Choosing Civility—The 25 Rules of Considerate Conduct* (St. Martin's Press, 2002). Regardless of whether we are in sync with the persons with whom we have relationships, being civil means considering and respecting their feelings, which might require our personal sacrifice, expressed through self-restraint. Dr. Forni says, "Life is what our relationships make it."

Civility is a useful tool to help improve the quality of everyday relationships in business. If we are to have harmonious interactions with our colleagues, clients and customers, our behavior must be guided by certain standards of decency. The three "R" principles—Respect, Responsibility and Restraint—are key to civility and are central to the way we relate to each other. If we want to have positive relationships, applying the three Rs is an important first step. For example, your clients would certainly rather hear a voice message saying that you are on vacation with your expected return date than be puzzled about why you have not returned their phone calls.

Why Focus on Civility?

Everyone, regardless of age, creed or position on a company's organizational chart can apply the three "R" principles in their relationships with others. The rules outlined in Dr. Forni's book serve as a set of tools to shape the outcome of our business and personal interactions. Showing respect for a client's time, acknowledging when our performance fails to meet expectations, observing company rules and policies, and giving credit to a colleague for a job well done are important. These acts of civility enhance and elevate our personal and professional image and help build strong relationships. Productive hours are lost in the workplace when employees are either absent or underperforming because of stressful or negative relationships with colleagues or management. Anger, frustration, or mean-spiritedness are unproductive and could even promote ill health.

Let's Be Civil

Rudeness and inconsiderate acts flourish every day, everywhere. Incivility rears its ugly head to create unpleasant or unacceptable situations with acts that intrude upon our lives as we travel on airplanes, roads and trains, or sit in boardrooms and classrooms. Failing to acknowledge a co-worker, shifting blame, giving destructive criticism, or indulging in gossip are common incivilities in today's business environments. Unwillingly, we have learned to go along with these unacceptable behaviors even though they may impair relationships, or limit our potential growth or that of a co-worker. The following questions can serve as a quick test of where you are on the civility scale:

The Civility Challenge Quiz

1. Do you ever type on the computer while talking with your clients or colleagues?

2. Have you ever cut someone off in traffic?

3. Have you ever taken credit for someone else's work?

4. Do you ever talk or text on your cell phone during meetings?

5. Have you ever been impolite to a service employee in a restaurant?

6. Have you ever failed to acknowledge a colleague?

If you answered yes to any of these questions, I encourage you to focus on embracing civility in your professional behavior and communication. If you answered yes to two or more of these questions, you may be civility-challenged. Your career could be suffering from a lack of civility and you may not even be aware of it.

The good news is that the three "R" principles provide a prescription for transforming lives positively, and can change negative behaviors, creating better relationships in both personal and professional settings.

The model below shows the interrelationships between each of the three "R" principles and the ABCs of image. Relationships are at the center of the model because they are central to business and to life. The rules of considerate conduct at the base of the model are directly related to image and civility. Considerate acts of kindness, giving, caring, taking care of your appearance, being a good guest and respecting others' space and time elevate and enhance your personal and professional image. Showing up to a business reception in tattered blue jeans or a strapless dress shows disregard for the hosts, the other guests and the venue owners. Project a more confident image by paying attention to the written or unwritten business rules of attire.

The Image and Civility Model

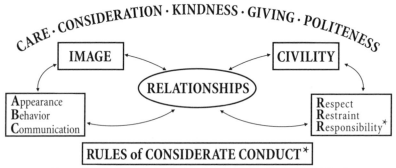

*Appears in *Choosing Civility—The 25 Rules of Considerate Conduct* by P.M. Forni

The 25 Rules of Considerate Conduct*

1. Pay attention
2. Acknowledge others
3. Think the best
4. Listen
5. Be inclusive
6. Speak kindly
7. Don't speak ill
8. Accept and give praise
9. Respect even a subtle "no"
10. Respect others' opinions
11. Mind your body
12. Be agreeable
13. Keep it down
   (and rediscover silence)
14. Respect others' time
15. Respect others' space
16. Apologize earnestly
17. Assert yourself
18. Avoid personal questions
19. Care for your guests
20. Be a considerate guest
21. Think twice before asking for favors
22. Refrain from idle complaints
23. Accept and give constructive criticism
24. Respect the environment and be gentle to animals
25. Don't shift blame and responsibility

* *Choosing Civility—The 25 Rules of Considerate Conduct* by Dr. P.M. Forni (St. Martin's Press, 2002)

Ethics and Integrity—The Heart of Civility

What is ethics, and what are its implications for your career? Civility embraces ethics. By providing helpful instructions to ensure that the customer's package would reach its destination on-time and intact, the Post Office employee mentioned in the opening paragraph of this chapter acted ethically by following the rules and doing the right thing. His actions were also in accord with the *Standards of Ethical Conduct for Post Office Employees:*

". . . employees are expected to become familiar with the laws and regulations applicable to their duties and to use their best efforts to comply. . . with all laws, rules and regulations applicable to the U.S. Postal Service's business."

A code of ethics is simply a system or collection of rules or standards that govern conduct in business. In the book, *Ethics 4 Everyone—The Handbook for Integrity-Based Business Practices* (The Walk the Talk Company, 2002), the authors Eric Harvey and Scott Airitam point out that all ethical decisions begin with the individual. The choices you make determine your standard of ethics and the ultimate effect of your company's codes of conduct.

Ethics scandals are in evidence all over the world. Unethical conduct may include accepting exorbitant gifts from business interests who seek special favors in return, plagiarism, or failing to disclose a financial connection that could compromise your professional judgment. Harvey and Airitam note, however, that most of the time, people are fair, honest and abide by the rules. However, an occasional misstep in judgment can be a disaster for one's reputation or career, given the image- and brand-driven focus of today's global business environment, and the prevalence of the Internet. A good example is Eliot Spitzer, former Governor of New York, whose alleged misdeeds forced him to step down from his office in disgrace.

Observance of the code of ethics is a key factor in employee performance evaluations and in maintaining a high standard of professionalism. Whether or not there is a code of ethics in your company or organization, ethical behavior is a measure of your personal and professional integrity and is of paramount importance to your success.

Knowing the Rules and Regulations

Before you can make a decision to act ethically, you must first know the relevant rules and regulations. I always stress to my clients that ignorance is no excuse for breaking the rules. Although we all have a basic sense of right and wrong that has been instilled since childhood, everyone should learn the culture of the company or organization in which they work. It is harder to be derailed by unethical conduct if your business decisions are guided by rules, laws and procedures. Trust, honesty, responsibility and respect are values that many businesses embrace.

Ethical decision-making must also be guided by doing the right thing, which is infinitely harder than not. We may observe a colleague misrepresenting his or her credentials to a client or seeking a special favor from a vendor for a family member—and yet we fail to take action. Since ethical dilemmas stem most often from issues that are not black-and-white, this poses challenges for employees and business owners.

How do we know what to do when faced with a potential ethics issue? Our stress-filled business world is influenced by peer pressure and the desire for quick success; it is so easy to abandon ethical conduct in favor of personal gain.

Complete the following checklist of questions before you make a decision about an ethical challenge. This could be the acid test that saves your reputation or career. The questions are adapted from *Ethics 4 Everyone—The Handbook for Integrity-Based Business Practices* by Harvey and Airitram, described on the previous page.

The Ethics Action Quiz

1. Is it consistent with the rules, laws and procedures?

2. Is it consistent with personal and organizational values?

3. Will it create a guilty conscience in me if I do it?

4. Is it consistent with stated commitments and guarantees?

5. Does it pass the "sniff" test?

6. Would the most ethical person I know take this action?

If your response to one or more questions was no, you may want to revisit the code of ethics or seek appropriate guidance.

As with civility, ethics in business is all about the three "R"s. The key to business success is learning and practicing these principles and following the rules, procedures, and your internal value system.

Civility, image and ethics go hand-in-hand. There is no better executive image you could strive for than becoming known by your clients and colleagues as always civil and ethical, that you can be taken at your word and respected for your actions.

YASMIN ANDERSON-SMITH, MCRP, AICI FLC
KYMS Image International, LLC

Helping people, companies and organizations embrace civility, reshaping image, brand and style

(866) 247-4079
yasmin@kymsimage.com
www.kymsimage.com

Yasmin Anderson-Smith is president of KYMS Image International, a consulting firm specializing in personal and corporate image and brand management, etiquette, civility and youth empowerment. Yasmin brings vision, creativity, passion, and elegance to her seminars and workshops and has authored educational resource materials for etiquette and civility training. After more than fifteen years in management, Yasmin successfully transitioned her marketing, customer relations, training and communication skills into entrepreneurship.

A graduate of the London Image Institute, Yasmin frequently presents on image, etiquette, civility and personal branding in local and international settings. Currently, Yasmin chairs the Civility Project committee for the Association of Image Consultants International, and serves as etiquette and civility editor of *Image Update,* the magazine published by AICI. Yasmin's leadership and expertise underlie her commitment to enrich, elevate, encourage, empower and inspire all her clients.

More Executive Image Power

Now that you have all you need to know to truly build your best executive image, the next step is to take action. Get started on your own by applying what you have learned in the pages of this book.

We want you to know that we are here to help you meet your objective.

Below is a list of where we are located throughout the U.S. and Canada. We provide a variety of services and you can find out more about each of us by reading our bios at the end of our chapters, or by visiting our websites. For your convenience, we are listed below by geographic area.

When you are ready for one-on-one image consulting from any of the co-authors in this book—we are available! Call one of us in your area, let us know you read our book, and we will provide you with a free phone consultation.

Arkansas

Kathryn Lowell, AICI CIP   www.imagemattersgroup.com

California

Colleen Abrie, AICI FLC, CDI   www.colleenabrie.com

Jennifer Bressie   www.shoppersf.com

Betty Chu, AICI FLC   www.classinstyle.com

California (continued)

Julie Kaufman, MBA, AICI FLC	www.juliekaufman.com
Maureen Merrill	www.harrismerrill.com
Beth Thorp, AICI CIP, CMB	www.powerfulimpressions.net
Divya Vashi	www.imagedivya.com
Cynthia Bruno Wynkoop, Esq.	www.wynkoopimage.com

Georgia

Peggy M. Parks, AICI CIP	www.theparksimagegroup.com

Indiana

Beverly G. Samuel, MS, AICI FLC	www.phoeniximageinstitute.com

Maryland

Yasmin Anderson-Smith, MCRP, AICI FLC	www.kymsimage.com

New York

Lauren Solomon, MBA, AICI CIP	www.lsimage.com
Brenda Moore-Frazier, MS	www.signatureperformance.net

Missouri

Ginny Baldridge, AICI FLC	www.yourstyleginny.com

Pennsylvania

Suzanne Mauro, AICI FLC	www.suzannemauro.com

CANADA

Alberta
Joanne Blake, AICI CIP   www.styleforsuccess.com

Ontario
Karen Brunger, BHEc, AICI CIP   www.imageinstitute.com
Amy Elizabeth Casson, AICI FLC   www.polishedimage.com
Anne Sowden, AICI CIP   www.hereslookingatyou.ca

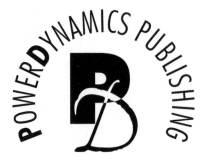

PowerDynamics Publishing develops books for experts who speak and want to share their knowledge with more and more people.

We know getting a book written and published is a huge project. We provide the resources, know-how and an experienced team to put a quality informative book in the hands of our co-authors quickly and affordably. We provide books, in which our co-authors are proud to be included, that serve to enhance their business missions.

You can find out about our projects at
www.powerdynamicspub.com